Language Matters

Language and Literature Skills for the new English Leaving Certificate Syllabus

Michael Smith

Edco
The Educational Company of Ireland

First published 1999

The Educational Company of Ireland
Ballymount Road
Walkinstown
Dublin 12

A trading unit of Smurfit Ireland Limited

Acknowledgments:
The publishers would like to thank the following for their permission to reproduce copyright material:
HarperCollins for *Angela's Ashes*, Frank McCourt; George T Sassoon and Barbara Levy for 'Suicide in the Trenches', Siegfried Sassoon; Liam Wright, Evening Herald for 'Getting the Tools for the Job', Patrick Ryan; William Reville for 'Time and Change'; The Irish Times for 'Boxing', Steven Young; 'Lost Children', Polly Devlin; Penguin for *Entertaining Mr Sloane*, Joe Norton; Faber and Faber for 'Servant Boy', Seamus Heaney; Cassell plc for 'The Habit of Reading', Richard Aldington (from *Life for Life's Sake*); J M Dent for 'A Refusal to Mourn the Death by Fire of a Child in London', Dylan Thomas (*Dylan Thomas: The Poems*, edited by Daniel Jones); Holt Rinehart and Winston Inc. for 'After Apple-picking', Robert Frost, (from *Complete Poems of Robert Frost*); Heinemann for *The World of Science*; F. Sherwood Taylor; Harcourt, Brace & World for *Oedipus Rex* (from *The Oedipus Cycle*, translated by Dudley Fitts and Robert Fitzgerald)

The publishers would also like to thank the following for permission to reproduce photographic material:
Mr Ian Spanton, Walker Books Ltd, for the Walker Brothers advertisement, 'Reading Together', The Eastern Health board for 'Don't Quit Quitting'.

If the publishers have inadvertently overlooked any copyright holders, they will be happy to make the appropriate arrangements at the earliest convenience.

Editor: Clare Rowland
Design and layout: Design Image
Colour: Impress Communications Limited
Printed in Ireland by

0123456789

**Printed in the Republic of Ireland by
Criterion Press Limited, Dublin.**

CONTENTS

FOREWORD

Language Matters is intended for both Higher and Ordinary Level students of the new Leaving Certificate English syllabus. All uses of language are explained and illustrated with a variety of examples, to enable the teacher to select the material most appropriate and helpful to his/her class.

For the same reason, Questions in general throughout the book are of different levels of difficulty. Furthermore, rather than explicitly categorising each question as of higher or ordinary level of difficulty, the writer has anticipated that the individual teacher would prefer to exercise his/her own judgement as to suitability.

Language Matters could be profitably used for one or two class periods per week throughout Fifth and Sixth Years. It provides comprehensive preparation for Paper I of the new Leaving Certificate examination as well as helping the student to acquire the literary skills which will be necessary for Paper II.

The essays on pages 16 and 65 are for Higher Level only.

THE USES OF LANGUAGE

1. THE LANGUAGE OF INFORMATION

Language can be used to communicate information: to give instructions, to set out or define an idea, to explain an event, a character or a situation. This use of language should strive to be non-emotional and impartial. It is the language of good reporting or recording. It should have no hidden agenda, message or moral. It should concern itself exclusively with 'facts'.

EXAMPLE

Coal can be turned into gas in various ways, the simplest of which is to heat it. Watch a lump of coal when put into the fire: it gives out smoke which later catches alight and burns with a bright flame. This smoke is very impure coal-gas. After a time no more flame comes from the coal and it simply burns with a bright red glow. If a bit of this glowing coal is quenched in water, you will see that it is coke.

from *The World of Science* by F. Sherwood Taylor

COMMENT

This passage describes the process by which coal is turned into coke. It is purely factual in its use of language and it communicates no emotion which the writer may have felt on observing the process. Its purpose is purely to communicate objective knowledge.

2. THE LANGUAGE OF ARGUMENT

This use of language is intended to change the reader's mind or point of view by the use of logical argument. Its essential appeal is to reason, intelligence or common sense.

❰ EXAMPLE

If, as many sociologists argue, unemployment and poor social conditions are mainly responsible for the epidemic of crime that rages in the Western World today, how is one to explain that in many periods in the past, as in Europe of the 1930s, when unemployment was so much greater than it is today and when the living conditions of the majority of the people were so much worse than they are today, crime was proportionately so much less? And if the sociologists have got it wrong, as seems to be the case, what then are the new factors, apart from unemployment and poor social conditions, that will explain the enormous rise in crime in our time? Is it not that sociologists in their analysis of the causes of crime do not concern themselves with moral values, with the 'right' and the 'wrong' of human behaviour, and instead confine themselves entirely to materialistic factors such as the lack of money, poor housing, illiteracy, etc.?

❰ COMMENT

The writer of this passage wishes to argue the reader into accepting the view that crime is not altogether caused by material social conditions but has 'moral causes'. The writer uses historical comparison as the main argument, arguing that if terrible social conditions in the past did not result in widespread crime, then the blame cannot now be placed on social conditions. There is, however, a flaw in the writer's argument, which the writer senses by concluding the paragraph with a question rather than a statement. A valid or at least convincing comparison requires like to be compared to like. But the social conditions of the past, taken as a whole, cannot be the same as those of the present if only because the present is a product of the past, has been altered by it and therefore is bound to contain new elements. The social conditions of any society at a given time, however similar to those of another time, cannot be exactly the same.

3. THE LANGUAGE OF PERSUASION

The purpose of this use of language is to convince or persuade the reader that a certain point of view, a certain way of looking at something, is right or wrong. It can involve information and argument, but it operates on the assumption that the end or objective (that is, changing the reader's point of view) is justified by any means the writer may employ. It can operate at an intellectual as well as an emotional level. Its success is entirely a matter of getting the reader to see and accept something in a certain way. This use of language is often that of advertising and politics.

EXAMPLE

I had never before seen anyone quite so ugly. His pig-like eyes stared beadily from the bulging globe of flesh that was his face. His mouth was small, with viciously thin lips that scarcely seemed to move as he spoke. One felt the effort words had to make as they emerged from that mouth. His laughter, if one may call it that, usually caused by some else's misfortune, was a hideous cackle.

COMMENT

The writer of this passage wishes to persuade the reader that the person being described is revolting. The writer uses the unpleasant associations of 'pig-like' and the metaphor of a 'globe of flesh' to suggest a monstrously fat face. The image of the mouth as 'small' and the lips as 'viciously thin' is intended to convey the feeling of meanness and spitefulness. The laughter of the person is described as a 'hideous cackle' in order to suggest the stereotypic image of the ugly witch of fairy-tales.

4. THE LANGUAGE OF NARRATIVE

Language can be used in the telling of stories, the description and explanation of human actions or behaviour. This use of language attempts to give meaning to our experiences, to explore and make sense of what we do. It concerns itself with what happened, why it happened, how it happened. It involves character, motivation, situation, conflict.

EXAMPLE

It was a dark autumn night. The old banker was pacing from corner to corner of his study, recalling to his mind the party he gave in the autumn fifteen years ago. There were many clever people at the party and much interesting conversation. They talked among other things of capital punishment. The guests, among them not a few scholars and journalists, for the most part disapproved of capital punishment. They found it obsolete as a means of punishment, unfitted to a Christian State, and immoral. Some of them thought that capital punishment should be replaced universally by life-imprisonment.

'I don't agree with you,' said the host. 'I myself have experienced neither capital punishment nor life-imprisonment, but if one may judge a priori, then in my opinion capital punishment is more moral and more humane than life-imprisonment. Execution kills instantly, life-imprisonment kills by degrees. Who is the more humane executioner, one who kills you in a few seconds or one who draws the life out of you incessantly, for years?'

from 'The Bet' by Anton Chekhov

❰ COMMENT

The writer presents a time, a setting, some characters and a situation. It is 'a dark autumn evening'. The old banker is speaking to a group of people whom he has invited to his house and whom he presumably knows. The banker raises the topic of capital punishment. This, as the writer well knows, is always a contentious topic. The old banker makes the seemingly outrageous statement that capital punishment is preferable to, more humane than life-imprisonment. What is his motive in expressing this obviously controversial view? What will the effect of this be on his guests? A story is about to unfold.

5. THE AESTHETIC USE OF LANGUAGE

The study and appreciation of the uses and techniques of language as a human activity in its own right without reference to some other practical end or objective is what is usually understood as literary aesthetics. It is the study and appreciation of the styles and techniques of a literary work whether it is a novel, short story, drama, poem or essay. This is language as play, as a non-utilitarian or non-practical activity, a delight in language for what it is in itself, the appreciation of language as something pleasurable in itself without consideration of it as, for instance, preaching a moral or demonstrating a theory.

However, modern linguistics has shown that there is no such thing as a neutral language, not even in the area of scientific writing. Language is a human creation and will always reflect a certain way of seeing the world. Thus the world or worlds of language cannot be said to correspond or refer to an objective world 'out there' that exists independently of language. Therefore all uses of language, including the aesthetic, must be read critically, that is to say with an awareness of the limitations and constraints of language as a 'conductor' or 'mediator' of 'reality'.

(A) POETRY

The essential difference between the language of poetry and language used in other ways is that the language of poetry has its primary value in **how** it is used rather than in **what** it says.

EXAMPLE

> The girl in the tea shop
>> Is not so beautiful as she was,
> The August has worn against her.
> She does not get up the stairs so eagerly;
> Yes, she also will turn middle-aged,
> And the glow of youth that she spread about us
>> As she brought us our muffins
> Will be spread about us no longer.
>> She also will turn middle-aged.

'The Tea Shop' by Ezra Pound

COMMENT

The poet wishes to comment on how fleeting physical life is. He does this, however, not by plain factual statement or heavy moralising, but by the presentation of carefully selected images: the not-so-young waitress, encroaching frailty, the autumn season of decline in nature, a reminder of the waitress's youthful past.

(B) FICTION

The language of fiction is emotive rather than factual, connotative rather than denotative. Language is used to convey feelings, atmosphere, mood rather than describe things objectively.

EXAMPLE

The weather had turned so much worse that the rest of the day was certainly lost. The wind had risen and the stormed gathered force; they gave from time to time a thump at the firm windows and dashed even against those protected by the veranda their vicious splotches of rain. Beyond the lawn, beyond the cliff, the great wet brush of the sky dipped deep into the sea. But the lawn, already vivid with the touch of May, showed a violence of watered green; the budding shrubs and trees repeated the note as they tossed their thick masses, and the cold, troubled light, filling the pretty drawing-room, marked the spring afternoon as sufficiently young.

from *The Story In It* by Henry James

◖ COMMENT

The writer of this passage is primarily concerned with describing a special setting and an atmosphere for his story. He is describing a special spring afternoon. He creates a sense of defensive cosiness by describing how the rain strikes against the windows in 'vicious splotches'. The rain-filled sky is presented as 'a great wet brush'. Even the lawn outside is pictured as 'a violence of watered green'. The wind-wracked shrubbery and trees are seen as tossing their 'thick masses' and the light outside is 'cold' and 'troubled'. By contrast with all of this outside elemental force and violence, the drawing-room is described as 'pretty', which carries with it the suggestion of something orderly and delicate.

(C) DRAMA

The language of drama takes the form of dialogue, speech used by characters in a situation of conflict. To be effective, it must accommodate visual elements such as theatrical props, cinematic devices, etc. Drama, or a play or film, is basically the exploration and presentation of human conflict within the context of theatre or cinema. The word 'human' gives us **characters** (actors, dialogue, settings of time and place, etc.) and 'conflict' gives us **action** (the response of characters to situations of conflict in which they find themselves).

The essential difference between the language of drama and other uses of language as in the novel (with which drama shares so much) is that drama is theatrically enacted human conflict. Whereas the novel has its readers, its literary portraits, its descriptive settings of time and place and its literary devices, drama has its actors and an audience. There is an essentially different relationship between the reader and the written word and an audience and dramatic performance.

EXAMPLE

The following is the opening scene from Joe Orton's *Entertaining Mr Sloane*:

A room. Evening.
[KATH *enters followed by* SLOANE]

KATH: This is my lounge.

SLOANE: Would I be able to use this room? Is it included?

KATH: Oh, yes. [*Pause*] You musn't imagine it's always like this. You ought to have rung up or something. And then I'd've been prepared.

SLOANE: The bedroom was perfect.

KATH: I never showed you the toilet.

SLOANE: I'm sure it will be satisfactory. [*Walks around the room examining the furniture. Stops by the window.*]

KATH: I should change them curtains. Those are our winter ones. The summer ones are more of a chintz. [*Laughs*] The walls need re-doing. The Dadda has trouble with his eyes. I can't ask him to do any work involving ladders. It stands to reason.

[*Pause*]

SLOANE: I can't give you a decision right away.

KATH: I don't want to rush you. [*Pause*] What do you think? I'd be happy to have you.

[*Silence*]

SLOANE: Are you married?

KATH: [*Pause*]: I was. I had a boy ... killed in very sad circumstances. It broke my heart at the time. I got over it though. You do, don't you?

[*Pause*]

SLOANE: A son?

KATH: Yes.

SLOANE: You don't look old enough.

[*Pause*]

KATH: I don't let myself go like some of them you may have noticed. I'm just over ... As a matter of fact I'm forty-one.

[*Pause*]

SLOANE [*briskly*]: I'll take the room.

from Entertaining Mr Sloane by Joe Orton

COMMENT

Two characters, Kath and Sloane, enter a scene which is simply described as 'a room'. The time is evening. Within one brief exchange between the characters we are presented with a situation: Kath is the prospective landlady, Sloane the inspecting, prospective lodger. Kath is keen to impress Sloane. Sloane is not fussed but is taking his time looking around at what is on offer. Will Sloane take the room? Will he be put off by the landlady's patter? What kind of relationship will develop between Kath and Sloane if Sloane decides to rent the room? Here we have dialogue, character, a setting and a developing situation. As this is merely the opening of the play, there is little or no tension, but an action of some sort is imminent.

SUBJECTIVE (EMOTIVE) AND OBJECTIVE (FACTUAL) USE OF LANGUAGE

In practice, language usually mixes the many uses outlined above. However, in order to study the techniques or genres of language it is useful to take clear-cut examples of all of these uses and to analyse how they function. But before doing this, a basic difference between two uses of language should be studied.

Language may be subjective or objective, emotive or factual. If we say that a tree in our garden is 'a silver birch, 12 years old and 13 metres in height' we are making an objective statement that can be *proved* to be either true or false. On the other hand, if we say that the tree is 'a lovely tree that adds a pleasing variety to the garden's greenery' we are not so much describing the tree, as it exists objectively, independently of us, as expressing *how we feel* about it. Another person may feel quite differently about the same tree. The ability to distinguish between objective and subjective statements or descriptions is essential to all good reading and writing, and it is also the measure of our literary skills.

CONNOTATIONS AND DENOTATIONS

Perhaps the most manageable way to understand the difference between the emotive and factual uses of language is to recognize that emotive language makes more intense and various use of the *connotations* or associations of words, which are the principal means of conveying feeling. By contrast, what a word *denotes* or defines is its dictionary meaning, what it refers to objectively or factually.

Words can convey a great deal more than their dictionary meanings. For example, if we look up the dictionary for the meaning of the word 'cat', we will find 'A carnivorous quadruped, *Felis domesticus*, which has long been domesticated'. Now for the word to communicate generally, we must all agree on this definition. But the word also carries other associated meanings which are called connotations. Some readers will imagine a certain breed of cat, of a certain colour or size; some readers will think of the quality of slyness or cunning; some readers will think of a folktale such as Dick Whittington and his Cat; others will think of witches and sinister things; or some readers may think of a purring fluffy kitten they were once given as a pet.

The poet as well as the copywriter in an advertising agency or the speechwriter for a politician, even more than the novelist or short-story writer, will manipulate these associations or connotations to convey feelings or emotions.

TEST YOUR READING SKILLS

Using the categories outlined above, identify and comment on the use of language in the following passages:

1. The storing of electricity is a great field for inventors. The lead accumulator is very efficient — you can get back almost all the electricity you put in — but it has several thoroughly bad features. First of all, it is very heavy. This makes it nearly useless for anything that has to move. A few electric vans run by batteries are used, chiefly because they pay a low tax, are very free from noise and vibration and stop and start very easily: but it is wasteful for a five-ton lorry to carry a ton and a half of accumulators as its source of power. Moreover, storage batteries are slow to charge, for electricity can only be put in at a certain rate. Lastly, they are rather short-lived.

2. It was late in November 1456. The snow fell over Paris with rigorous, relentless persistence; sometimes the wind made a sally and scattered it in flying vortices; sometimes there was a lull, and flake after flake descended out of the black night air, silent, circuitous, interminable.

To poor people, looking up under moist eyebrows, it seemed a wonder where it all came from.

3. The true vampires are bats which feed upon the blood of animals, their extremely sharp teeth enabling them to make an incision in the skin without the animal feeling it. The bat approaches its sleeping victim silently, alights nearby and walks or runs towards it. Having penetrated the skin, the blood begins to flow and is licked up by the tongue, coagulation being prevented by certain liquefying properties in the saliva. Horses, cattle, sheep, pigs and poultry are attacked, as well as human beings who may chance to sleep out of doors, loss of blood causing weakness and emaciation. The true vampire bats, which occur in Brazil, are quite small and without tails. There are several species of so-called vampire bats, but apparently only very few that actually suck blood.

4. This cat I am going to tell you about is a very small cat, and in fact it is only a few weeks old, consequently it is really nothing but an infant cat. To tell the truth, it is just a kitten.

It is grey and white and very dirty and its fur is all frowzied up, so it is a very miserable-looking little kitten to be sure. Today it crawls through a broken basement window into an old house in East Fifty-third Street over near Third Avenue in the city of New York and goes from room to room saying merouw, merouw in a low, weak voice until it comes to a room at the head of the stairs on the second storey where a guy by the name of Rudolph is sitting on the floor thinking of not much.

5. The greatest punishment God can inflict on the wicked, is when the church, to chastise them, delivers them over to Satan who, with God's permission, kills them or makes them undergo great calamities. Many devils are in woods, in waters, in wildernesses and in dark pooly places, ready to hurt and prejudice people. Some are also in the thick black clouds which cause hail, lightnings and thunderings, and they poison the air, the pastures and grounds. Physicians say it is natural, ascribing it to the planets, and showing I know not what reasons for such misfortunes and plagues as ensue.

6. The Inca of Peru was its sovereign in a peculiar sense. He received an obedience from his vassals more implicit that that of any despot; for his authority reached to the most secret conduct — to the thoughts of the individual. He was reverenced as more than human. He was not merely the head of the state, but the point to which all its institutions converged, as to a common centre — the keystone of the political fabric which must fall to pieces by its own weight when that was withdrawn. So it fared on the death of Atahuallpa. His death not only left the throne vacant, without any certain successor, but the manner of it announced to the Peruvian people that a hand stronger than that of their Incas now seized the sceptre, and that the dynasty of the Children of the Sun had passed away forever.

7. For many purposes it is essential to maintain the temperature constant at a given value or within given limits, and for many others it is a great convenience to be able to do so. It is not possible, however, to maintain the temperature constant at a desired value for long periods of time without some form of automatic control. An instrument that performs this service is termed a thermostat.

8. Of the dealings of Edward Bellingham with William Monkhouse Lee, and of the cause of the great terror of Abercrombie Smith, it may be that no absolute and final judgment will ever be delivered. It is true that we have the full and clear narrative of Smith himself, and such corroboration as he could look for from Thomas Styles the servant, from the Reverend Plumptree Peterson, Fellow of Old's, and from such other people as chanced to gain some passing glance at this or that incident in a singular chain of events. Yet, in the main, the story must rest upon Smith alone, and the most will think that it is more likely that one brain, however outwardly sane, has some subtle warp in its texture, some strange flaw in its workings, than that the path of Nature has been overstepped in open day in so famed a centre of learning as the University of Oxford.

9. A whale, being a mammal, breathing by means of lungs, has to return to the surface at frequent intervals although it may descend to great depths to obtain food. On breaking surface, the first thing it does is to discharge the air contained in its body in order to take in

a fresh supply. This issues forth at considerable pressure from its one or two blow-holes or nostrils controlled by valves which are situated on the top of the head. This air or breath, being at a high temperature, condenses on coming in contact with the outside air and so forms a great column of visible vapour. When a whale is said to spout it is not throwing up a fountain of water, but hot breath. The Whalebone or Baleen Whales have two blow-holes, the Toothed Whales only one.

10. In the middle of the night I woke from a dream full of whips and lariats as long as serpents, and runaway coaches on mountain passes, and wide, windy gallops over cactus fields, and I heard the man in the next room crying, 'Gee-up!' and 'Whoa!' and trotting his tongue on the roof of his mouth.

   It was the first time I had stayed in grandpa's house. The floor-boards had squeaked like mice as I climbed into bed, and the mice between the walls had creaked like wood as though another visitor was walking on them. It was a mild summer night, but curtains had flapped and branches beaten against the window. I had pulled the sheets over my head, and soon was roaring and riding in a book.

11. I knew a simple soldier boy
   Who grinned at life in empty joy,
   Slept soundly through the lonesome dark,
   And whistled early with the lark.

   In winter trenches, cowed and glum,
   With crumps and lice and lack of rum,
   He put a bullet through his brain.
   No one spoke of him again.

   · · · · · · · ·
   You smug-faced crowds with kindling eye
   Who cheer when soldier lads march by,
   Sneak home and pray you'll never know
   The hell where youth and laughter go.

   'Suicide in the Trenches' by Siegfried Sassoon

THE LANGUAGE OF
INFORMATION

NEWSPAPER REPORTS, ARTICLES, ESSAYS

Factual or informational writing is primarily concerned with explaining a subject. Its intention is to give information. It uses description, comparison and contrast.

A writer may wish to explain how a machine works, how the market economy functions in certain conditions, or the current state of a political situation in some part of the world.

Purely factual writing tries to be objective. Its virtues should be clarity of expression and comprehensiveness of presentation.

THE FACTUAL REPORT OR ARTICLE

At least some of the following questions are usually answerable from a good piece of expository writing:

WHAT?

What is the nature of the object, idea, situation, etc.?

What uses does it have?

WHERE?

Where did it originate?

WHO?

Who invented, discovered, created, devised, the subject?

WHEN?

What is its historical context?

HOW?

How does the object, system, etc. work?

The following example of not-too-technical informational writing is from a gardening column of a popular evening newspaper. The writer is giving advice on the purchase and maintenance of garden tools. He is answering the questions of WHAT to buy. It is written in easy conversational language for the non-expert. It is informational writing for popular consumption.

GETTING THE TOOLS FOR THE JOB by PATRICK RYAN*

Buying garden tools can be an expensive business, but it doesn't have to be that way. Many people seem to get somewhat carried away by the sheer size and variety of the range of tool available and buy all those which they *think* they'll need, only to find out later that they could have done without some of them.

In fact, the list of recommended garden tools is actually quite a short one: spade, fork, hoe, rake, trowel, hand-fork, secateurs, watering can and a thick pair of gardening gloves. As far as larger items go, the only two that most people need are a lawnmower and wheelbarrow.

Armed with all of these, you'll be equipped to tackle just about any garden job that crops up.

Avoid the common mistake of buying the least expensive tools that you can find in a bid to save money — it's a false economy. Although there's nothing wrong with shopping around for a bargain, if you cut corners by purchasing lesser quality tools, you'll find that they don't last very long and will soon need replacing.

Look for tools with sturdy wooden handles and make sure that the metalwork is stainless steel, as it is rust-resistant and much easier to keep clean. In the case of secateurs, again you should buy the best that you can afford.

The blades of cheaper, inferior quality secateurs have a tendency to move out of alignment, and the subsequent loss in their performance can lead to damaged plants as they crimp and tear rather than cut cleanly.

---

*from *The Evening Herald*, March 17, 1995

To prolong the lives of your tools, keep them inside whenever they're not in use (leaving them out in the rain is a recipe for disaster) and don't put them away without thoroughly cleaning them first. You should always sharpen blades regularly and give them a light application of oil from time to time. The effort is well worth it. If you look after your tools, they'll reward you with a lifetime of service.

The following is a piece of technical informational writing for young people. The writer is intent on not overwhelming his young writers with too much technical data.

◀ DESTINATION MARS by DAVID C KNIGHT*

The possibility of life on the other planets in our solar system has fascinated Man for centuries. Of all the planets, Mars has been considered to be the one must likely able to support some form of life.

Although it is somewhat smaller than the Earth, Mars resembles the Earth in several ways. For example, the Martian day is only a few minutes longer than the 24-hour Earth day. Also, the axis of Mars is tilted at an angle of 24 degrees in its orbit, as compared with $22^1/_2$ degrees for Earth. This means that Mars has seasons like the Earth does. There are seasonal variations in surface features on Mars that could be caused by vegetation of some kind growing in the spring and dying in the autumn.

There are also, of course, significant differences between Mars and the Earth. For example, the Martian year is almost twice as long as the Earth year, and, being much farther away from the Sun, Mars is a lot colder than the Earth is.

Mars is too far away from us to be able to distinguish any detailed features. With the naked eye, it appears just as a bright, reddish star. Through a telescope you can see that it is a disk. And you can distinguish lighter and darker areas. But that is all. What is the actual surface really like?

No one knew until 1965. In July of that year an American space probe, Mariner IV, passed a little over 6,000 miles away from the surface. Then, in a fantastic feat of communications, it transmitted the photographs slowly

---

*from *The First Book of Mars* by David C Knight (Franklin Watts, London and New York)

back to Earth 135 million miles away. The photographs were startling. They revealed a totally bleak and barren landscape covered in craters like the Moon is. This view of Mars was confirmed four years later when two more American space probes, Mariners VI and VII, passed even closer to the planet and took photographs.

In the light of the findings of the Mariner probes, our ideas about Mars have radically altered. There seem to be no signs on any of the photographs of anything that might suggest the presence of life. The conditions on Mars have been shown to be so harsh that even the most primitive organisms known on Earth could not possibly survive.

● EXERCISES

Write informational pieces on the following:

1. The history of your favourite sport	11. The motor car
2. Travel	12. Pollution
3. Cinema	13. The computer
4. Pop music	14. Democracy
5. Global warming	15. Money
6. The industrial revolution	16. Capital punishment
7. The city	17. The game of chess
8. The drug culture	18. The feminist movement
9. Television	19. The fridge
10. The fashion industry	20. Architecture

● FACTUAL ARTICLES

HIGHER LEVEL ONLY

❰ TIME AND CHANGE by DR WILLIAM REVILLE*

The most fundamental explanation of the physical world is supplied by physics. Many familiar and seemingly simple things turn out to be difficult to understand at a fundamental level. Several week ago I wrote about the puzzling nature of light. Today I will consider the nature of time and, specifically, why it moves forward. To understand this requires a little pondering, but it is fun.

*The Irish Times, Oct. 19, 1998

First of all, let me digress slightly from the orderly sequence of my story.

Consider the following problem. You are shown two photographs — one of an egg, and another of a scrambled egg — and you are asked to place them in correct time-sequence. No prizes for getting this right. The egg always comes first. In the real world a scrambled egg never turns into an unscrambled egg. Even if you assembled a crack team of scientists, and asked them to assemble eggs from scrambled eggs, they would fail. Unless of course they had secret knowledge, which I will reveal at the end of this article.

Time marches forward. We all know this. You are born, you grow old, and you die. The classical physical explanation for the arrow of time comes from the second law of thermodynamics. This law states that all spontaneous change in a closed system occurs in such a manner as to maximise the entropy (disorder) of the system, i.e., maximising disorder imposes a direction on change. Thus, for example, if you place two bodies in contact, one hot and one cold, heat always flows from the hot to the cold body. The temperature of the hot body drops and that of the cold body rises until they are both equal, at which point heat flow stops.

In the above example, the starting situation, where the heat is segregated from the cold, is more orderly than the final state where the heat is randomly distributed between the two bodies. If you were shown photographs of the two states you could unerringly choose the one that comes first in temporal sequence. You know that two objects in contact and each at the same temperature never spontaneously behave so that heat flows from one to the other resulting in an end-state of a hot block in contact with a cold block. Things always move in a certain direction, in temporal sequence, and the direction of the temporal sequence is the arrow of time.

But why does heat flow from hot to cold? Both bodies in the above example are composed of atoms and heat is determined by how fast the atoms vibrate.

Atoms in the hot body vibrate faster than atoms in the cold body. At the interface between the two bodies the faster-moving hot atoms collide with the slower-moving cold atoms, sharing energy with them. The faster atoms are slowed down and the cold slower atoms are speeded up. You can see how this transfer of energy at the interface will gradually spread out through both bodies, slowing down the atoms in the hotter block and speeding up the atoms in the cooler block until eventually all atoms in both blocks are vibrating at about the same rate.

Now, why does the situation never spontaneously reverse itself? It could in theory but it never does in practice. Atoms bump into each other all the time. You can imagine a situation where an atom is hit from behind, receiving an impetus in its direction of motion and speeding it up. By chance it keeps getting bumped in the rear in its direction of motion and vibrates faster and faster.

Exactly the same thing could happen by chance to about half the atoms at the interface between the two bodies, resulting in an undirectional transfer of heat. This could continue to happen by chance at the interface, resulting in a shunting of heat from one block to the other, eventually restoring the initial condition whereby most of the atoms on one body are vibrating faster than the atoms in the other, and again we have a hot body in contact with a cold body.

This could happen, but it is easily appreciated that it is just about infinitely improbable. The probability that the random collisions of the atoms will perpetuate the averaged-out homogeneity of the state where the two blocks are at the same temperature is vastly greater that the probability of one alternative scenario developing as described above.

It is all a matter of probability. Imagine an assembled jig-saw puzzle in a box. Shake the box vigorously and the puzzle breaks up. Continue shaking it and it breaks into smaller and smaller segments. Will the pieces every reassemble into a completed puzzle?

In practice — no. There is an extremely tiny chance that, on one shake, all the pieces will fall together just the right way to complete the puzzle. But this can happen only one way. The number of incorrect ways the pieces can relate to each other is so vastly greater than the one correct way that, in practice, the puzzle will never spontaneously reassemble.

In the ordinary world of experience time moves forward. However, the rate at which time passes depends on the speed at which the observer is moving. The faster you move the slower time passes, but it only really becomes noticeable if you travel at a large fraction of the speed of light. If you could actually reach the speed of light, which is impossible, time would stand still.

Now, as a reward for sticking with me to the end I will reveal the secret of how to unscramble eggs. Take some hens and starve them of solid food for one day to ensure their stomachs are empty. Now feed them on scrambled eggs. Wait for 1–2 days, and voilà!

● QUESTIONS

1. Explain in your own words what William Reville is attempting to demonstrate in this article.

2. How effective are the two comparisons of the scrambled eggs and the jigsaw puzzle in explaining the writer's ideas? Say what you think these ideas are.

3. How would you describe the writer's attitude towards his readers? Granted that the article appeared in a fairly popular non-specialist newspaper, does it presume too much knowledge on the part of its readers?

4. How successfully or otherwise does the writer communicate the factual information that is the substance of his article?

5. Do you think that the writer might have made his treatment of his article more accessible to the non-scientific reader? How do you think he might have done this?

6. What methods are used by the writer to accommodate his non-scientific readers? Give examples in your answer.

◀ THE WORLD OF THE OCEAN by SAMUEL W MATTHEWS*

The world ocean. It blankets seven-tenths of the earth, salt bitter, oft storm racked, most of it pitch dark and near freezing. Averaging two and a half miles deep the world around, it holds, by some estimates, 99% of the life-supporting space on our planet.

It separates the great landmasses of the globe, affects their weather, provides their life-sustaining rain, receives their off-flowing waters — and poisons. It surges to the pull of the moon and sun, swirls to the spin of the earth, and carries in its currents the energy of solar heat and the chill of polar ice.

I have lived beside the sea, sailed upon it by catboat and Navy cruiser, crossed the Atlantic, Pacific and Indian Oceans, flown above the Arctic, and dived to the floor of the Caribbean Sea in a tiny submersible.

* from *National Geographic*, Dec. 1981

Nonetheless I *know* almost nothing deep and certain about the ocean. Its essence is immensity, and mystery, and power.

So it is to most of us, even in the heyday of science. Man has lived by the ocean and voyaged upon it for thousands of years. Yet only in the past three decades, one human generation, have we begun to see, to map, and dimly to comprehend the true nature, shape, and complexity of the world ocean. It is a startling prospect indeed.

In 1950, only a few years after World War II, Rachel Carson published *The Sea Around Us*. She told of what science knew then about the ocean — its origins, currents, unseen depths, and strange life forms. But many a chapter of her evocative review ended on a similar note: 'At present we do not know ... No one can say.'

By 1981 many of those blanks were being filled in. Instruments not even invented three decades ago now measure the vast movements and forces at work in the ocean. Undersea vehicles carry explorers thousands of feet deep to towering mountain ranges and yawning rift valleys. Satellite sensors and seismic stethoscopes take the pulse of the earth itself.

Consider just a few of the things we now know about the ocean, after these 30 historic years of exploration:

- The seafloor — that nearly 72% of the planet's crust covered by salt water — has been 'seen' with sound waves and mapped in fine detail for the first time.

- The seabed is constantly being created and destroyed; the oceans are opening or closing; the continents around them are drifting, carried on giant rafts. New crust oozes up in molten form from below, solidifies, and moves outward; old, cold crust dives into deep trenches and is reabsorbed into the interior of the earth.

- As the seafloor splits and moves apart, earthquakes jar the planet and volcanic mountains grow in the ocean. Minerals are born and deposited in the seabed: oil beneath deep sediments, metals from spewing hot springs, others from seawater itself.

- Ocean waters flow and overturn in unsuspected ways, carrying energy absorbed from the sun, regulating the earth's daily weather and long-term climate. They wash away — and ominously retain — man's most dangerous wastes. They nurture blooms of microscopic life, meadows of drifting plankton, entire fisheries.

● Life, which began in the sea, still reveals new and wondrous forms there, from bacteria flourishing in utterly dark depths to larvae of fish and crustaceans nourished in sun-blessed shallows, from myriad krill and anchovies to territorial sharks and intelligent porpoises and gentle, singing whales, largest of earth's creatures.

Man's driving curiosity about what lies in and under the oceans is nothing new, of course. We inherit it from our earliest human ancestors who ventured to catch and eat a fish, open an oyster, or drift out from shore upon a floating log.

● QUESTIONS

1. How does the writer generate interest in the topic of his article?

2. How would you describe the tone of this article?

3. How does the writer convince the reader that he is an authority on the subject of his article?

4. How would you describe the style of writing used in the article? Use quotations to illustrate your analysis.

5. Give in your own words the main points made by the writer.

THE BOOK REPORT

A book report should be primarily descriptive, not evaluative. Evaluations are more the business of literary criticism. Nevertheless, a book report will usually say whether the author has succeeded or failed, and why.

The following questions should be answered in a comprehensive book report:

1. The name of the author? Nationality? Period of history? Cultural context?

2. Other works by the same author?

3. Anything special in the circumstances of the writing of this particular book?

4. What kind of book is it? What genre does it belong to?
   Fiction?   Biography?
   Drama?   Travel?
   Poetry?   Sport?
   History?

5. What is the subject matter of the book?

6. What is the theme or main idea of the book?

7. How does the author deal with the material? What is its principle of organisation?

8. How would you describe the tone and style of the book?

EXAMPLE OF A BOOK REPORT

Title: *Portrait of T E Lawrence*

Author: Vyvyan Richards

This is a biography of T E Lawrence, the liberator of Arabia, translator of Homer's *Odyssey*, ascetic, archeologist, soldier and writer of the monumental *Seven Pillars of Wisdom*. Richards was a personal friend of the hero, although he was not an intimate friend as Lawrence was so reserved a person that scarcely any of his friends may be described as intimate.

Richards, like all the biographers of Lawrence, suffers from a huge initial disadvantage: that of having to retell what Lawrence himself has already so well told in his *Seven Pillars of Wisdom*. Richards does his best to cope with this by compressed summaries, abundant quotation of original texts and by enlightening those years of Lawrence's life which the great man himself glossed over or ignored.

Richards writes with restraint. He avoids the temptation to sensationalise or glamorise a subject that so easily lends himself to that treatment.

EXERCISES

Write a book report on:

1. A best-selling novel you have read recently
2. A travel book
3. An autobiography
4. A true-life story
5. A history book
6. A classic novel you have read
7. A book on your favourite author
8. A book you have studied for a project
9. A book on a film or pop star
10. A science book

THE NEWSPAPER REPORT

The key questions which a good newspaper report of an event should answer are:

WHAT was the nature of the occasion? An accident? A public demonstration? A strike?

WHERE did the event occur? Town, region, country?

WHEN did the event occur? Day, date, time?

WHO was involved in the event? Names of people? In what capacity?

HOW did the event occur? Objective description.

EXAMPLE OF A NEWSPAPER REPORT

(This is adapted and abbreviated from an actual article which appeared in *The Irish Times*.)

Factory to close with over 100 job losses

The 120 workers in the Supersoft textile plant in Galway are to be made redundant tomorrow, it was announced last night, as talk with Forbairt aimed at securing a buy-out package by management and workers failed.

Reacting to the news, the Minister for Enterprise and Employment, Mr Jones, said he was disappointed that the company had gone ahead with voluntary liquidation.

With officials in his Department and Forbairt, Mr Jones added, he had invested significant time and commitment over recent weeks to secure the future of the company.

'Intensive last-ditch endeavours were made to find a commercially viable solution. Regrettably, one could not be found,' he said, adding that the emphasis now would be on finding a replacement industry for the textile plant.

Forbairt said that a detailed analysis of the proposed buy-out had shown that it was not a commercial proposition. This was due to a variety of factors, including critical commercial deadlines — a reference to the warning of two major customers that they would have to go elsewhere if the company's difficulties had not been resolved by yesterday.

Last night a trade union official said the mood at the plant was one of 'harsh disappointment'. He said that he believed the cash short-fall was not sufficiently serious to justify the closure of the plant.

● EXERCISES

Write a newspaper report on the following:

1.	A court case	7.	An industrial dispute
2.	An accident	8.	A criminal occurrence
3.	A public demonstration	9.	A financial crisis
4.	A natural disaster	10.	A Budget announcement
5.	A political event	11.	An athletics meeting
6.	A public scandal	12.	A soccer match

WHAT SHOULD OR SHOULD NOT BE PRINTED IN A REPORT AS RECOMMENDED TO JOURNALISTS IN DEMOCRATIC COUNTRIES.

1. The press will do all in their power to ensure that the information imparted by them to the public is factually accurate. They will check before publishing all items of information to the best of their ability. No facts are to be wilfully distorted or essential facts deliberately suppressed.

2. The right of the individual to protection of his reputation and integrity shall be respected. Publicity that violates the sanctity of privacy shall be avoided, unless it is deemed necessary in the interest of the public.

3. If and when an inaccurate or false piece of information is published, the paper concerned shall correct it at the earliest opportunity, giving the correction the same prominence as the earlier incorrect information.

4. News reports shall be strictly separated from opinion. The opinion of a writer may only be included in the news when it carries his/her by-line.

5. Discretion must be observed concerning sources of information. Professional secrecy must also be observed in all matters revealed in confidence.

6. In reporting crime stories it must be solemnly observed that the accused is innocent until he or she is found guilty by a competent court of law.

7. The personnel of the press must never accept any form of bribe or permit personal interest to influence their sense of justice and impartiality.

8. Newspapers shall not deliberately or calculatedly incite religious or racial hatred or subject any race, religion, or nationality to unjust criticism.

9. Nothing shall be published that will endanger the security of the state, stability and sovereignty of the Union.

10. Commercial announcements or advertisements in the form of news articles, pictures, and features must be published in such a way as to leave no doubt that they are commercial announcements or advertisements.

11. The following are to be avoided in any form of publication such as articles, news items, or photographs etc.:
    (a) Immorality or obscenity
    (b) Use of vulgar expressions
    (c) Malicious imputations
    (d) False and defamatory statements.

● QUESTIONS

1. Which of these rules do you consider to be most important? Give reasons for your answer.

2. Which of these rules do you consider to be most breached? Why do you think this is so?

3. Do you think any of these rules interfere with the freedom of the press and therefore should be amended or scrapped?

4. Write an essay on the importance of the press in a free society.

THE LANGUAGE OF PERSUASION

Advertising is big business. It is a huge industry in itself as well as a service to industries of every sort. It can also be a small company catering for small and even personal businesses. So far as we are concerned here, the focus of attention is on advertising in NEWSPAPERS and MAGAZINES and in the form of POSTERS.

WHAT IS ALLOWED

- Advertising is controlled by the law (statutory regulation) in the matter of tobacco, medicines and medical services, credit agencies (banks, etc.) and employment. Advertisers who break the law can be fined and suffer other penalties.

- Advertising is also controlled by the Advertising Standards Authority of Ireland (ASAI) in the case of all other consumer items and services.

- Basically, the ASAI is a watchdog committee funded by the advertising and media agencies. It operates a code of advertising standards. Its job is to see that advertisements are not deliberately misleading and respect the rules of fair play and competition. The ASAI is independent of the Government, it has no force of law and it exercises its power by influence.

- The Complaints Committee of ASAI consists of eleven members. Of these only three are drawn from the professional and media workforce.

- The Complaints Committee accept complaints, investigate them and if necessary invite the advertisers to consider the complaints. These complaints are reported on and it is clearly in the interest of advertisers NOT to be involved in any complaints because of the possibility of bad publicity.

A CRITICAL GRID

In order to respond critically (as we should) to an advertisement, we should keep in mind the following questions. These questions taken together form a kind of grid through which an advertisement can be filtered so that we are not deceived or misled by advertisers. Given the influence of advertising, such a protection is almost a necessity of modern life. We have to learn how to 'read' advertisements, to become advertising-literate.

CRITICAL GRID

WHO? is selling WHAT? HOW? and TO WHOM?

WHO

- **CLIENT**
  Industrial producers of any commodity such as a car manufacturer, services companies like banks, charities, political parties, religions, etc.

- **ADVERTISING AGENCY**
  A company that contracts with the client to promote the sale of a product, an idea or a message through the use of the resources of the advertising medium, dependent upon the amount of money the client is prepared to spend on the promotion.

- **SELLING**
  The word 'selling' as used here should be understood as meaning not only 'selling' in the literal sense, but also **'persuading'**.

WHAT

The product or idea or service to be promoted.

HOW?

Choosing the place of appearance of the advertisement.

Designing an effective advertisement to appear in that place.

TO WHOM?

The target audience or potential market to be reached by the advertisement.

> Having briefly defined the terms above, we must now consider them in greater detail and also examine how they work together. We can begin with the last.

TO WHOM? TARGET AUDIENCE

Although the client and the client's money is ultimately the most important factor, it is the advertising agency that decides HOW and TO WHOM. Let us first look at the target audience.

The nature of the target audience decides WHERE the advertisement will appear (in which paper or magazine, and also HOW the advertisement will be designed (for example, an advertisement designed for *The News of The World* will be different from one designed for *The Sunday Times*).

The advertising agency analyses the product (whether it be a consumer item or a 'message') and decides what kind of people are likely to be persuaded to buy it. As a help to them in working this out, people have been grouped into several groups according to income, interests and lifestyle. These socio-economic groups are rated from A to E, with E standing for the lower end of the income scale.

A = The well-to-do
B = The middle class
C = The lower middle class
D = The working class
E = The poor

A more old-fashioned system would be like the following, which is worth giving here if only because it gives some indication of the considerations that go into classifying the target audience.

1. Universal mass market: men and women, all areas, all age groups.

2. Upper class market: men and women, all areas, all age groups, but upper third of the population.

3. Well-to-do market: men.

4. Housewives: mass appeal.

5. Housewives: upper middle class appeal.

6. Well-to-do market: women.

7. Young people (men and women aged 16–24): mass appeal.

8. Young women (aged 16–25).

9. Specialist groups: professional, retail trade, occupational, hobby, etc.

10. Older people (over 40, men and women): mass appeal.

HOW? TECHNIQUES OF ADVERTISING

In designing an advertisement, whether for newspaper, magazine or poster, the various specialists working in the advertising agency are concerned with the following:

1. **Copy** (textual matter):
   - **headlines or slogans: rhymes, puns**
   - **typographic (print) design or layout: large print, small print, italics, capital letters**
   - **statistics**
   - **factual information**
   - **endorsements or testimonials**
   - **emotive language**

2.   **Visual image:**
   ● **photographs**
   ● **artwork:** logo (symbol of client company or product), drawings

3.   The **relationship** of the copy to the visual image (how they work together)

In Detail

When writing about advertisements and judging their effectiveness, you will need to be able to comment on the above. In order to do this, you need to know more about these matters.

THE HEADLINE OR SLOGAN

The purpose of a headline or slogan is to fix the advertisement in the memory of the reader.

To do this the writer of the headline often uses rhymes (for example, mat/cat), puns (that is, words that play on two or more meanings).

For instance: *For an open and shut case, choose XXXX* ('case' here means both 'briefcase' and law 'case'), assonance (vowel rhyme: for example, father/ far) and alliteration (syllables beginning with the same consonant: for example, We take the trouble, You take the trip).

An effective headline should be
● memorable (catchy)
   For example: **A Mars a day helps you work, rest and play**

● make an offer of some kind (for example, a discount or trade-in)
   For example: **Fifty fifty cash back**

● offer some immediate benefit (for example, by responding now you get something for nothing)
   For example: **Book now and one passenger goes free**

● indicate the price (if it is tempting)

● tie-in with the advertisement's artwork

Of course, not all headlines achieve all of these aims, but it is still worth bearing in mind what the writers of headlines are hoping to achieve.

TYPOGRAPHY (PRINT)

Readability is the gauge of good typographic layout. The choice and arrangement of the print should help the reader to get the 'message' which is the purpose of the advertisement. It has been proved, for instance, that text or copy set completely in capital letters is more difficult to read that copy which uses both capital and lower case type. Large type may be striking to the eye, but it must also pass the test of readability.

Blocks of small type are a deterrent to the reader, so it is considered a good idea to break the copy into small paragraphs, preferably separated by cross-heads (headings in large or different type).

In the case of special offers, advertisers often conceal or play down, by the use of very small type, conditions attaching to the special offer (for example, that you must buy the item advertised before a special date to avail yourself of the special offer). So when an advertisement contains a special offer, the reader needs to be extra vigilant in responding to it.

Trick or gimmicky typography may be very eye-catching, but to be really effective it needs to do more than attract attention: it must also communicate.

Some typefaces are more elegant than others, so the typeface should suit the product.

STATISTICS

Statistics can be very effective in persuading people to buy a product or agree with a viewpoint. We tend to place our trust in the belief that most people cannot be fooled all of the time. Statistics is also an instrument of science and carries the authority that scientific statement usually has for us.

However, when considering the use or misuse of statistics, it is important to enquire about the source of the statistics. Who has compiled them? What interest has that person or company in the findings of the statistics? If an advertisement for a dairy product (for example, cheese or butter) quotes a set of statistics which indicates that there is no necessary connection between the consumption of dairy products and heart attacks, the reader must find out if the dairy industry itself carried out the survey, or whether it was carried out by an impartial body such as a university medical department.

FACTUAL INFORMATION

Factual information, like statistics, can be very influential in persuading the potential consumer. The advertiser, however, is legally bound not to tell lies or deliberately misrepresent the product being advertised. An advertisement for a lotion claiming, as a matter of fact, to cure baldness, would be misleading: it is well known that hair cannot be regrown except by a process of hair-transplanting. However, many advertisements for cars state as a matter of fact that the car can travel at so many kilometres per litre. What such advertisements fail deliberately to mention is that such fuel consumption is conditional on a traffic-free road and a facing wind-velocity below average.

The rule to use in judging the factual content of an advertisement is that of the legal formula of 'the truth, the whole truth and nothing but the truth'. Half the truth may be a lie, and leaving out some factual information may amount to a distortion of the truth tantamount to being a lie. The key question to ask in judging the factual content of an advertisement is its reliability. On whose authority is the factual information based? Is that authority a respected one? People often believe what they want to believe, contrary to their common sense.

ENDORSEMENTS OR TESTIMONIALS

Endorsements or testimonials can be very effective. The most balanced view on testimonials is that of David Ogilvy, one of the great figures of modern advertising. 'Testimonials from celebrities,' writes Ogilvy, 'get high recall scores, but I have stopped using them because readers remember the celebrity and forget the product. What's more, they assume that the celebrity has been *bought*, which is usually the case. On the other hand, testimonials from *experts* can be persuasive — like having an ex-burglar testify that he had never been able to crack a Chubb safe.'

The non-expert celebrity's testimonial of a product contributes to the name of the brand and helps to keep the brandname in public consciousness. But it is the qualification of the expert that ultimately persuades the consumer to buy a product. The endorsement of a car by a famous Formula One driver is likely to be more persuasive than that of a film star who has no known expertise on cars.

EMOTIVE LANGUAGE

Words not only denote, that is, have a dictionary meaning, but they also connote or carry associated meanings. The dictionary will denote the meaning of the word 'dog', but for one person the word will be accompanied by images of a poodle or a dearly loved black and white mongrel, while for someone else, it has associations of a fierce German shepherd dog that once scared him or her half to death.

Writers of advertising copy, just like poets and novelists, carefully calculate the connotations or associations of words. Their intention will be to associate the product being advertised with very pleasant things or with unpleasant things, as the case may be. The following is the copy of the famous Charles Saatchi on the importance of food hygiene. Saatchi wanted to associate poor hygiene with unpleasantness:

> **This is what happens
> when a fly lands on your food.**
>
> **Flies can't eat solid food,
> so to soften it up they vomit on it.
> Then they stamp the vomit in
> until it's a liquid, usually stamping in
> a few germs for good measure.
> Then when it's good and runny
> they suck it all back again, probably
> dropping some excrement at the
> same time.
> And then, when they've finished
> eating, it's your turn.**

THINGS TO CONSIDER WHEN WRITING ABOUT ADVERTISEMENTS

When responding to an advertisement, in newspaper, magazine or poster form, the following considerations should be kept in mind.

Not all of these apply to every advertisement.

1. Identify the **target audience** of the advertisement.

2. Write comments on the **copy** of the advertisement under the following headings:

   (a) headline

   (b) typographic design or layout

   (c) statistics

   (d) factual information

   (e) endorsement or testimonial

   (f) emotive language

3. Comment on the **visual image**.

4. Write three or more sentences on the way the copy, layout and visual image combine to achieve a certain purpose. Say what that purpose is.

5. What in your opinion is the value of the **endorsement?**

● RESPOND TO THE FOLLOWING ADVERTISEMENTS, USING THE ABOVE HEADINGS

PR (Public Relations)

In modern times, almost all businesses — industrial, commercial, service — require the assistance of Public Relations to conduct their businesses successfully. One has only to think of the use made of PR companies by governments, tourist organisations, the world of entertainment and banks.

PR companies may be very large, employing many people and huge budgets, or consist of individuals who usually specialise in the world of popular entertainment.

The essential difference between a PR company and an advertising agency is that the advertising agency operates through *paid* advertisement, whereas the PR company operates through the *editorial* channels of newspapers, magazines, radio, television (i.e. the mass media), feeding information and 'news' stories to reporters, journalists and columnists. This can be viewed as 'free' advertising, although the PR company

DON'T QUIT QUITTING

Trying to quit smoking? Finding it tough? Wait. Don't give up: research shows that those who successfully quit smoking have tried many times. Each attempt is important to reach that goal of a smoke free life.
The Eastern Health Board can help you quit or cut down - we can provide individual counselling for smokers trying to quit. We also run smoking cessation support groups throughout Dublin, Wicklow and Kildare.
For more information contact your local health centre or The Eastern Health Board Health Promotion Department, 15 City Gate, St. Augustine St., Dublin 8. Ph: 01- 670 7987
Don't quit quitting: your next try may be your last.

EASTERN HEALTH BOARD

may reward the person who uses the PR material with some kind of perk; for example, an airline company or travel agency may offer a free flight to a holiday resort.

As well as trying to get favourable publicity for a client, the PR company may also have the task of trying to prevent a client from receiving bad or unfavourable publicity.

PR companies usually operate

though hand-outs. These are prepared 'stories' or 'news' items that easily slot into certain newspaper, magazines, etc. Readers of these 'stories' are usually not aware that the journalist or columnist has been 'fed' this information by the PR company. For the journalist under pressure or the lazy journalist, these hand-outs can be very welcome, an easy way of filling space. An efficient PR company depends on useful contacts with people in the media, and it will cultivate the goodwill of these people in every way possible.

The way a PR company operates can be very clearly seen in the case of the promotion of an entertainer or celebrity. Say, for example, a pop star is due to give a concert in a couple of months. Over that period the PR company will 'feed' stories to the mass media about that star, having the star mentioned whenever and wherever possible. Then, as the date of the concert approaches, the PR publicity machine functions with increased energy. The star's name appears with ever greater frequency and in more and more outlets. The idea behind this strategy is to make the public feel that a great event is about to happen, an event that 'everyone' is talking about, an event not to be missed. The public perception would be that if the mass media are showing such interest in this event, it MUST be important. The reality is that the PR company, operating behind the scenes, has been orchestrating the whole thing.

For this reason it is important that we should make ourselves aware of the possibility of a PR company being at work in the promotion of any product or service or idea. We should make ourselves aware of a newspaper's or journalist's use of the hand-out material of a PR company. We should make ourselves aware that what seems to be straight reporting may in fact be the highly biased presentation of someone or something by a PR company.

QUESTIONS TO ASK WHEN CRITICALLY READING A PASSAGE OF PERSUASIVE PROSE

WHAT IS THE SUBJECT MATTER?

The difference between **subject matter** and **theme**:

The **subject matter** is the raw material the writer is using (the factual information referred to in the passage). For example, the subject matter of a novel may be 'life on a working-class housing estate' or 'the lives of nurses and doctors in a general hospital'.

The **theme** or **intention** is the use the writer is making of the raw material to persuade the reader to a certain point of view. For example, the theme of the novel may be 'crime does not pay' or 'we must take responsibility for our own lives'. Theme is what we usually mean by a 'moral' or a 'message'.

The **subject matter** is to the **theme** what **clay** is to the **vase** which the potter makes of it.

EXAMPLE

A few days ago the writer of a letter to a daily newspaper raised, in a new form, an old, well-known cry: 'that familiar cry of the elderly, that the country, to judge from the behaviour of the young, was going to the dogs'. In this instance the evidence was the spelling. Undergraduates, we were told, cannot spell their own native tongue; they are totally unfamiliar with its structure; indeed, they have 'only the foggiest notion that English is something other than a loosely phonetic language'.

COMMENT

The subject matter of this passage is the English language. The writer clearly intends to discuss if and how knowledge of the English language has declined, as many older people seem to think. He will discuss such things as spelling and grammar.

● COMPOSITION

Identify the subject matter of the following passages:

1. 'It was some Englishmen who came to Beiginis,' and he looked out to Beiginis as he spoke. 'They had a big boat and they used to spend the week there fishing. That is why the old ruin is to be seen on the Island still. Well, Maurice, one day we were going out to Mass — the King, Seán Fada and I — and we were rowing at our ease past Beiginis to the north when my oar caught in a rope ...'

2. Yesterday I should have gone back to school, had I been a hundred years younger.

    My most frequent dream nowadays — or nowanights I suppose I should say — is that I am back at school, and trying to construe difficult passages from Greek authors unknown to me. That they are unknown to me is my own fault, as will be pointed out to me sternly in a moment. Meanwhile I stand up and gaze blankly at the text, wondering how it is that I can have forgotten to prepare it.

3. When William caught sight of the valley of the Boyne, he could not suppress an exclamation and a gesture of delight. He had been apprehensive that the enemy would avoid a decisive action, and would protract the war till the autumnal rains should return with pestilence in their train. He was now at ease. It was plain that the contest would be sharp and short.

4. When he first appeared, scarcely a foot long, his brow furrowed with loose wrinkles, as if he bore all the cares of the world upon him, Rufus looked like a bloodhound on an extremely reduced scale. Then he grew and grew longitudinally and emerged from the process as a dachshund of highly respectable pedigree and a pleasing brown colour. From his unpopularity with the other dogs in the village, it is believed that they do not recognise him as a fellow-dog and take him for some kind of rat.

5. The other day there was a ship that died. It was my own ship, and in a way I would it had not died. But die it had to, for it was mortal, having been made in this world: to be accurate, at Bembridge, in the Isle of Wight, nearly sixty years ago. Moreover, since boats also must die, it is right that they should die their own death in their own element; not violently, but after due preparation; for, in spite of modern cowardice, it is better to be prepared for death than unprepared.

WHAT IS THE INTENTION OF THE WRITER?

To **persuade** the reader to accept a certain viewpoint?

Is the writer **using language emotively** (that is, working on one's feelings) in order to prejudice or persuade the reader to think about something in a certain way?

What **images** is the writer using to persuade the reader?

Connotations: These are the meanings we associate with words besides their dictionary meanings.

For example, the use of the word 'tropical' to suggest exotic things such as sunshine and sandy beaches, warm blue seas, palm trees, adventure, faraway places.

Similarly, a writer may write 'He wallowed in self-pity' (using a metaphor with unpleasant associations, of a pig wallowing in the muck) to turn us against someone.

Connotations are used to work on our feelings or emotions, either to make us like or dislike.

WHAT IS THE ATTITUDE OF THE WRITER TOWARDS THE SUBJECT MATTER? (THIS DETERMINES THE TONE OF THE WRITING)

Serious?

Humorous?

Confident or authoritative?

Hostile?

Uncertain?

Sympathetic?

Respectful?

Condescending (treating the reader as inferior)?

Intimidating or bullying?

Belligerent or aggressive?

Exploitative or manipulative?

EXAMPLE

A few stars are known which are hardly bigger than the earth, but the majority are so large that hundreds of thousands of earths could be packed inside each and leave room to spare; here and there we come upon a giant star large enough to contain millions of millions of earths. And the total number of stars in the universe is probably something like the total number of grains of sand on all the seashores of the world. Such is the littleness of our home in space when measured up against the total substance of the universe.

COMMENT

The tone of this passage is serious but not heavy. The writer is confident in his knowledge of his subject matter. He doesn't overpower the reader with statistics and technical information, though the reader feels that he could if he wished.

EXAMPLE

When a woman says 'I look a fright' she invariably adds, by way of explanation, 'My hair is a show.' She is referring, not to a worsening condition due to the ravages of time, but to a temporary set-back due to want of time. She seems to be making a statement, but she is really planning a campaign.

COMMENT

The writer's attitude towards his readers is sexist. Women are seen as rather comical creatures who cannot recognise the difference between the triviality of a hairstyle and the seriousness of life. The writer feels that his male readers will share this view of women. Worse still, he seems unaware that this view is offensive to women and that he hasn't taken their feelings into account.

WHAT METHODS OR TECHNIQUES OF LANGUAGE ARE BEING USED BY THE WRITER?

Metaphors and similes are two important techniques of language used to influence the reader. Both are comparisons and they worked by bringing images of association into play.

metaphor: 'He was so hungry, he wolfed his food down.'
simile: 'He was ravenous as a wolf.'

The **difference** between a metaphor and a simile:

A simile is introduced by the words **like** or **as**.

A simile is a **more limited** comparison than a metaphor.

For example:

He fought like a lion. (This comparison tends to be limited to the bravery of the lion in fighting.)

He was a lion in the fight. (This comparison brings in not only courage, but wildness and strength, etc.)

EXAMPLE

But that was not the same snow. Our snow was not only shaken in whitewash buckets down the sky, I think it came shawling out of the ground and swam and drifted out of the arms and hands and bodies of the trees; snow grew overnight on the roofs of the houses like a pure and grandfather moss, minutely ivied the walls, and settled on the postman, opening the gate, like a dumb, numb thunderstorm of white torn Christmas cards.

COMMENT

The writer uses both metaphors and similes in this passage. The snow is 'shaken in whitewash buckets'; it 'shawls' and 'swims' and 'grows'; the trees have 'arms and hands and bodies'; it 'ivies' the walls. By using these metaphors, Thomas wants to convey the effect of countless white snowflakes swirling down from the sky and covering everything they fall on. Besides these metaphors, Dylan Thomas uses two similes: the snow covers the roofs of the houses like moss; and the postman, covered in snow, comes through the gate like a 'thunderstorm'.

The overall effect of these metaphors and similes is to enrich the description by bringing numerous images of association into play. For example, to say that the snow grows like moss, conveys not only a sense of softness and smoothness but also the way moss can cover over rough surfaces.

> **Use metaphors and similes in a description of a walk through a heavy downpour of rain.**

● EXERCISES

Say what the following **metaphors** add to the description:

1.   He had a mountain of problems facing him.

2.   He was a terrier in the ring.

3.   The cold bit into their hands.

4.   The sun was splitting the heavens.

5.   It was raining cats and dogs.

6.   The teacher is a mine of information.

7.   The smoke snaked across the sky.

8.   He was a fox among chickens.

9.   To bring Mary into that company was to put a fox among chickens.

10. She is a dove of peace.

● EXERCISES

Say what the following **similes** add to the description:

1.   She was as wise as an owl.

2.   The old man was as sly as a fox.

3.   The teacher was like a raging bull last Monday.

4.   The dress was white as snow.

5.   Her hair shone like gold.

6.   He roared like a lion.

7.   The girl swam like a fish.

8.   He ran like the wind.

9.   She was like a fish out of water.

10. He is as stubborn as a mule.

STEREOTYPING

A stereotype is a common type, based on abstraction. Common types are the miser, the bully, the racist, the love-sick teenager, etc. Although people in actual life sometimes conform to common type, usually they are more complex than this. Stereotypic characters are the stock-in-trade of television 'soaps' and popular fiction. They confirm our prejudices and add little or nothing to our understanding of human beings. They elicit a stock response. Stereotyping is often dangerous because it distorts life by over-simplification.

EXAMPLE

Stereotype of a football hooligan

He stood before me in an aggressive pose, his hands tightly clenched. His hair was cut to within a centimetre of his scalp. A small silver ring pierced his right nostril, and rings also dangled from his ear lobes. The red and white scarf of his team was wrapped twice around his bull neck. His fingers glittered with I don't know how many thick rings. He didn't so much speak as make menacing guttural noises.

COMPOSITION

Write a short description of stereotypes of the following:

1.	a bully	6.	a vulgar millionaire
2.	a pop star	7.	a nice old lady
3.	a miser	8.	a cranky shopkeeper
4.	a conceited pop star	9.	a yuppie
5.	a bored housewife	10.	a coward

HOW EFFECTIVELY DO YOU THINK THE WRITER HAS ACHIEVED THE OBJECTIVE OR OBJECTIVES OF THE PROSE PASSAGE?

To answer this sort of question, you must first of all work out the intention of the writer.

In so far as the writer has successfully carried out his or her intention, the passage may be said to be effective.

WHAT IS YOUR IMPRESSION OF THE WRITER?

This is a matter of style, of how the writer expresses him/herself.

What kind of person comes across to you from the passage?

Serious?	Depressing?
Humorous?	Interesting?
Cheerful?	Boring?
Optimistic?	Snobbish?

● QUESTION AND ANSWER

Describe the tone of the following passage:

St. Francis of Assisi was very fond of birds, and often had his picture taken with them sitting on his shoulders and pecking at his wrists. That was all right, if St. Francis liked it. We all have our likes and dislikes, and I have more of a feeling for dogs. However, I am not *against* birds as a class. I am just against pigeons.

I do not consider pigeons birds, in the first place. They are more in the nature of people; people who mooch. Probably my feeling about pigeons arises from the fact that all my life I have lived in rooms where pigeons came rumbling in and out of my window. I myself must have a certain morbid fascination for pigeons, because they follow me about so much — and with evident ill will. I am firmly convinced that they are trying to haunt me.

Although I live in the middle of a very large city (well, to show you how large it is — it is the largest in the world) I am awakened every morning by a low gargling sound which turns out to be the result of one, or two, or three pigeons walking in at my window and sneering at me. Granted I am a fit subject for sneering as I lie there, possibly with one shoe on or an unattractive expression on my face, but there is something more than just a passing criticism in these birds making remarks about me. They have some ugly scheme on foot against me, and I know it. Sooner or later it will come out, and then I can sue.

from *Of Pigeons* by Robert Benchley

❘ COMMENT

The tone of this passage is humorous. The main device of humour may be described as comic exaggeration. St Francis, for instance, is portrayed as a sort of tourist posing for a photograph with the pigeons perched on his shoulders.

The main exaggeration used is that of portraying pigeons as 'in the nature of people'. Out of this the writer develops further exaggerations.

These 'pigeon-people' are out to get the writer. They come to his window to sneer at him. They have 'some ugly scheme on foot' against him. The writer even considers suing them.

A FAMOUS PERSUASIVE SPEECH

Martin Luther King Jr. was born in Georgia in the United States in 1929 and he was murdered in 1968 in circumstances which are still controversial. At the age of eighteen he became an ordained minister. Having graduated from Moorehouse College, Boston University and Chicago Theological Seminary, King committed himself to the anti-racist struggle taking place in the USA in the sixties. In 1965 he became a national figure there through his leadership of the anti-segregationist demonstrations in Montgomery, Alabama. The Nobel Peace Prize was awarded to him in 1964. The following is his most famous address to the American people.

I HAVE A DREAM

I am happy to join with you today in what will go down in history as the greatest demonstration for freedom in the history of our nation.

Five score years ago, a great American, in whose symbolic shadow we stand today, signed the Emancipation Proclamation. This momentous decree came as a great beacon light of hope to millions of Negro slaves who have been seared in the flames of withering injustice. It came as a joyous break to end the long night of their captivity. But one hundred years later, the Negro still is not free. One hundred years later, the life of the Negro is still sadly crippled by the manacles of segregation and the chains of discrimination. One hundred years later, the Negro lives on a lonely island of poverty in the midst of a vast ocean of material prosperity. One hundred years later, the Negro is still anguished in the corners of American society and finds himself in exile in his own land. And so we have come here today to dramatise a shameful condition.

In a sense we have come to our nation's capital to cash a cheque. When the architects of our republic wrote the magnificent words of the Constitution and the Declaration of Independence, they were signing a promissory note to which every American was to fall heir. This note was the promise to all men — yes, Black as well as white men — that they would be guaranteed the inalienable rights of life, liberty and the pursuit of happiness.

It is obvious today that America has defaulted on this promissory note insofar as her citizens of colour are concerned. Instead of honouring this sacred obligation, America has given the Negro people a bad cheque, a cheque which has come back bankrupt. We refuse to believe that there are insufficient funds in the great vaults of opportunity of this nation; and so we have come to cash this cheque, a cheque that will give us upon demand the riches of freedom and the security of justice.

We have also come to this hallowed spot to remind America of the fierce urgency of *now*. This is no time to engage in the luxury of cooling off or to take the tranquilising drug of gradualism. *Now* is the time to rise from the dark and desolate valley of segregation to the sunlit path of racial justice. *Now* is the time to lift our nation from the quicksands of racial injustice to the solid rock of brotherhood. *Now* is the time to make justice a reality for all of God's children.

It would be fatal for the nation to overlook the urgency of the moment. This sweltering summer of the Negro's legitimate discontent will not pass until there is an invigorating autumn of freedom and equality. Nineteen sixty-three is not an end, but a beginning. And those who hope that the Negro needed to blow off steam and will now be content will have a rude awakening if the nation returns to business as usual. There will be neither rest nor tranquillity in America until the Negro is granted his citizenship rights. The whirlwinds of revolt will continue to shake the foundations of our nation until the bright day of justice emerges.

But there is something that I must say to my people who stand on the warm threshold which leads into the palace of justice. In the process of gaining our rightful place, we must not be guilty of wrongful deeds. Let us not seek to satisfy our thirst for freedom by drinking from the cup of bitterness and hatred. We must forever conduct our struggle on the high plane of dignity and discipline. We must not allow our creative protest to degenerate into physical violence. Again and again we must rise to the majestic heights of meeting physical force with soul force. And the marvellous new militancy which has engulfed the Negro community must not lead us to a distrust of all white people; for many of our white brothers, as evidenced by their presence here today, have come to realise that their destiny is tied up with our destiny, and they have come to realise that their freedom is inextricably bound to our freedom.

We cannot walk alone. And as we walk we must make the pledge that we shall always march ahead. We cannot turn back. There are those who are asking the devotees of civil rights, 'When will you be satisfied?' We can never be satisfied as long as the Negro is the victim of the unspeakable horrors of police brutality. We can never be satisfied as long as our bodies, heavy with the fatigue of travel, cannot gain lodging in the motels of the highways and the hotels of the cities. We cannot be satisfied as long as the Negro's basic mobility is from a smaller ghetto to a larger one. We can never be satisfied as long as our children are stripped of their selfhood and robbed or their dignity by signs stating 'For Whites Only'. We cannot be satisfied as long as the Negro in Mississippi cannot vote and a Negro in New York believes he has nothing for which to vote. No, no, we are not satisfied, and we will not be satisfied until justice rolls down like waters and righteousness like a mighty stream.

I am not unmindful that some of you have come here out of great trials and tribulations. Some of you have come fresh from narrow cells. Some of you have come from areas where your quest for freedom left you battered by the storms of persecution and staggered by the winds of police brutality. You have been the veterans of creative suffering. Continue to work with the faith that unearned suffering is redemptive.

Go back to Mississippi, and go back to Alabama. Go back to South Carolina. Go back to Georgia. Go back to Louisiana. Go back to the slums and ghettos of our Northern cities, knowing that somehow this situation can and will be changed. Let us not wallow in the valley of despair.

I say to you today, my friends, even though we face the difficulties of today and tomorrow, I still have a dream. It is a dream deeply rooted in the American dream. I have a dream, that one day this nation will rise up and live out the true meaning of its creed: 'We hold these truths to be self-evident, that all men are created equal.' I have a dream that one day, on the red hills of Georgia, sons of former slaves and the sons of former slave owners will be able to sit down together at the table of brotherhood. I have a dream that one day even the state of Mississippi, a state sweltering with the heat of injustice, sweltering with the heat of oppression, will be transformed into an oasis of freedom and justice. I have a dream that my four children will one day live in a nation where they will not be judged by the colour of their skin, but by the content of their character.

I have a dream today. I have a dream that one day down in Alabama — with its vicious racists, with its governor's lips dripping with the words of interposition and nullification — one day right here in Alabama, little Black boys and Black girls will be able to join hands with little white boys and white girls as sisters and brothers.

I have a dream today. I have a dream that one day every valley shall be exalted and every hill and mountain shall be made low, the rough places will be made plain and the crooked places will be made straight, and the glory of the Lord shall be revealed, and all flesh shall see it together.

This is our hope. This is the faith that I go back to the South with. And with this faith we will be able to hew out of the mountain of despair a stone of hope. With this faith we will be able to transform the jangling discords of our nation into a beautiful symphony of brotherhood. With this faith we will be able to work together, to play together, to struggle together, to go to jail together, to stand up for freedom together, knowing that we will be free one day.

And this will be the day — this will be the day when all God's children will be able to sing with new meaning:

> My country, 'tis of thee,
> Sweet land of liberty,
> Of thee I sing;
> Land where my fathers died,
> Land of the Pilgrims' pride,
> From every mountainside
> Let freedom ring.

And if America is to be a great nation, this must become true.

And so let freedom ring from the prodigious hilltops of New Hampshire. Let freedom ring from the mighty mountains of New York. Let freedom ring from the heightening Alleghenis of Pennsylvania. Let freedom ring from the snowcapped Rockies of Colorado. Let freedom ring from the curvacious slopes of California.

But not only that. Let freedom ring from Stone Mountain of Georgia. Let freedom ring from Lookout Mountain of Tennesse. Let freedom ring from every hill and molehill of Mississippi. 'From every mountainside let freedom ring.'

And when this happens — when we allow freedom to ring, when we let it ring from every village and every hamlet, from every state and every city — we will be able to speed up that day when all of God's children, Black men and white men, Jews and Gentiles, Protestants and Catholics, will be able to join hands and sing in the words of the old Negro spiritual: 'Free at last! Free at last! Thank God Almighty. We are free at last!'

● QUESTIONS

1. King makes extensive use of the connotative and metaphorical resources of language throughout his speech. Identify a number of examples of this use of language and discuss how they work.

2. King's speech deliberately employs a good deal of repetition of phrases. What is the intention of this repetition? Illustrate your answer with references to specific examples.

3. The tone of King's speech can be described as prophetic. How does King manage to give that tone credibility and authority?

4. Although King's speech is intended to be confrontational, it is also intended not to antagonise. How does the speech accommodate these two conflicting attitudes? Give examples in your answer.

5. King was a religious minister — an Evangelical preacher — by vocation. How does the speech show the influence of that?

6. Would you consider King's speech a successful piece of persuasive oratory, justifying its far-flung fame? Give reasons for your answer.

THE LANGUAGE
OF ARGUMENT

Before dealing with writing and criticising essays of any kind, it is worth considering what are the requirements for a good essay. The following list gives the main qualities that are taken into consideration in assessing an essay.

- **Interest and quality of content**
- **Novelty of treatment or approach**
- **The persuasive use of argument** (logic and use of evidence)
- **Relevance** (staying close to the essay topic)
- **Coherence** (how the parts of the essay bond together into a unity)
- **Constructive paragraphing**
- **Vocabulary** (range and accuracy in the use of words)
- **Grammar** (adherence to the established rules of grammar)
- **Sentence structure** (sentences that make sense, that contain a meaningful unity of thought or description, that are varied)
- **Spelling**
- **Punctuation**
- **Use of metaphors and similes**
- **Use of authorities and statistcs**

AN APPROACH TO THE ARGUMENTATIVE ESSAY

ARGUMENTS INVOLVE PROPOSITIONS

A **proposition** proposes or puts forward a statement as true or false. For example: War is evil. Or: There is life on Mars.

Essentially, there are **two kinds of proposition**:

1. A proposition arrived at by **Induction.**

A writer may propose a statement that is true or false as **a matter of fact.** Statements of this kind are said to be verifiable, that is to say, the truth or falseness of the statement can be determined by reference to factual or scientific knowledge. One can consult textbooks of accepted factual knowledge, reliable authorities or experts and statistics.

2. A proposition arrived at by **Deduction.**

A writer may propose a statement that is **a matter of duty or obligation.** Statements of this sort involve the words 'ought' or 'ought not', 'should' or 'should not'. For example: Children should respect their parents. This kind of statement is not a matter of fact but is arrived at by logical argument or deductive reasoning. This latter kind of reasoning will be explained later.

It is extremely important to distinguish between the two kinds of proposition.

STEP-BY-STEP METHOD FOR WRITING AN ARGUMENTATIVE ESSAY

Before writing

1. Analyse the essay topic and convert it into the form of a proposition.

2. Decide which of the two kinds of proposition you are going to put forward.

3. Decide whether your proposition will be (a) positive, (b) negative or (c) neutral (pure discussion).

Beginning to write

4. In your first paragraph (or two if necessary), establish the issue which the essay topic raises for you. You many choose to do this by referring to some recent event or happening. Formulate the proposition you are going to put forward.

5. They are three remaining steps to be completed in your essay:

    (a) You must set out the arguments which you anticipate will be set against your proposition, and you must counter these arguments. This is the negative or destructive part of your work. The more effective you counter the arguments against your proposition, and the stronger these arguments are, the more persuasive your own proposition is going to be. (This should take about two or three paragraphs.)

(b)   The next step in your essay is to present the positive arguments for your proposition. (This should take two or three paragraphs.)

(c)   This final step should take the form of a summary of your arguments and your counter-arguments. It should also show that you have dealt with the issue raised by the essay topic.

ESTABLISHING THE PROPOSITION IN ESSAY TOPICS

Essay topic: The cosmetic industry — boon or fraud?

Propositions: (a) The cosmetic industry should be outlawed if it can be established that it is a fraud, an industry based on lies and false claims; (b) The cosmetic industry is a worthwhile industry; it provides jobs, gives hope to many and represents the human struggle with ageing and death.

Essay topic: Is it right to experiment with animals?

Propositions: Human beings (a) should or (b) should not have the right — and (a) should or (b) should not be allowed — to experiment with animals for whatever purpose.

● ESTABLISH THE PROPOSITION(S) IN THE FOLLOWING ESSAY TOPICS:

1.   The school as it exists today is really a thing of the past. Education today needs a new kind of school.

2.   Technology, once the servant of human beings, is now their master.

3.   People nowadays opt for living so much in the present because they cannot bear to look into the future.

4.   The computer is replacing human intelligence.

5.   When people talk about progress they should not so easily assume that it is always a good thing.

6.   People in glass-houses shouldn't throw stones.

7.   Literature is dead! Long live the video!

8. Contact sports like football and boxing are no more than substitutes for the tribal warfare of the past.

9. Feminism has caused more problems than it has solved because it is based on false biology: that women can be men.

10. However unpleasant to think it, wars, famines and viral epidemics are necessary to keep the world's population under some kind of control.

PROCEDURE OF ARGUMENT

INDUCTIVE REASONING

Use of evidence

(a) **Factual or scientific evidence**. The truth or falseness of this kind of evidence can be checked against the authority of reputable experts or an accepted body of knowledge.

(b) Use of **evidence of opinion**. This kind of evidence is what a person believes personally to be true or false. It may be based on what the person has witnessed first-hand or has been told by someone else. The force and reliability of this kind of evidence depends on the reputation or authority of the person who holds the opinion. At any rate, it is not verifiable in the same way that factual evidence is.

DEDUCTIVE REASONING

Generalising: A large part of reasoning is conducted through generalisations. We use averages and probabilities.

Syllogistic logic: The use of the syllogism is an important part of the procedure of argument.

GENERALISING

As most arguments and attitudes are based on generalisations, we should be careful in our examination and use of them.

The validity of a generalisation depends on (a) how many specific cases have been observed (b) how representative these are, and (c) how reasonably the exceptions can be explained.

For example, if it happens that all the American people you have met have been loud-mouthed and aggressive, you may be inclined to generalise that all Americans are loud-mouthed and aggressive. In fact, you have probably met a mere handful of Americans and you have no idea whether or not even these few can be considered representative. Therefore any argument based on the assumption that all American are loud-mouthed and aggressive must be, to say the least, very inadequate and non-persuasive.

THE SYLLOGISM

The classic form of the syllogism is as follows:
Major Premise: All men are mortal.
Minor Premise: Socrates was a man.
Conclusion: Therefore Socrates was mortal.

When we examine this syllogism, we see that the Subject of the Major Premise ('All men') includes the Subject of the Minor Premise ('Socrates'), and that what is predicated or stated of both (they are both 'mortal') is the same thing. These are the conditions that must be met if the Conclusion is to be true or valid.

FALSE SYLLOGISM

The following would be an error in syllogistic logic:
Major Premise: Some men are tall.
Minor Premise: Socrates was a man.
Conclusion: Therefore Socrates was tall.

Clearly this is not a safe conclusion. The reason for this is that the subject of the major premise ('Some men') does not necessarily include the subject of the minor premise ('Socrates').

SOME MISTAKES IN REASONING

Begging the question
The mistake involved in this is to assume the truth of a proof which you are trying to establish.

For example:

A: I think that novel is a work of genius.

B: Why do you think that?

A: Because it impressed me enormously.

B: Why so?

A: Because it is a work of genius.

QUESTIONS

Give five examples of arguments that beg the question.

IGNORING THE QUESTION

This involves both a mistake in reasoning and is often a deliberately used tactic in debate. The idea is to shift the argument to a different issue.

The most frequent example of this is known in Latin as *argumentum ad hominem* ('an argument addressed to the person' rather than the issue of debate).

For example: A is arguing that unemployment causes crime. B points out that A personally has no experience of unemployment and therefore has no personal authority to speak about the issue.

QUESTIONS

Give five illustrations of ignoring the question.

NON SEQUITUR

'Non sequitur' is Latin for 'it does not follow'. This is a very common mistake. For example: Paul has attended a number of soccer matches at which there have been outbursts of hooliganism. He argues that it is the sport of soccer that incites people to hooliganism. Hooliganism is bad, therefore soccer is bad. But the second statement does not follow logically from the first one.

QUESTIONS

Give five examples of non sequiturs.

● QUESTIONS

Discuss the errors in the following arguments:

1. His generosity might have been inferred from his humanity, for all generous people are humane.

2. We respect those that keep us in order, and we respect those that shine at games; hence, it is a reasonable assumption that those who are good at games should be good disciplinarians.

3. Of course, the USA, though a mixture of races, is an Anglo-Saxon nation. All Anglo-Saxon nations are devoted to freedom, and devotion to freedom is nowhere more evident than in America.

4. These politicians are against a united Europe. Nationalists are against a united Europe. Hence, however much they deny it, these politicians are evidently nationalists.

5. A society which has lost its religion becomes sooner or later a society which has lost its culture.

A FEW BASIC RULES FOR WRITING ARGUMENTATIVE COMPOSITIONS

● **USE SIMPLE SENTENCES IN SO FAR AS POSSIBLE**

Do not write: The mechanic who was repairing my father's car told us that the car, which we had for twelve years, was too old and too unreliable for a long journey such as the one we planned to take to France, and that it would be better for us to hire a car there or replace the old one at whatever expense.

Suggested re-write: The mechanic who was repairing my father's car told us that it was too old and unreliable for a long journey. The car was twelve years old and it would not make the trip to France which we had planned. It would be better, he said, to hire a car there or replace the old one at whatever expense.

● **AVOID SLANG (UNLESS YOU INCLUDE A CHARACTER IN YOUR ESSAY WHO USES SLANG)**

Do not write: I let me teacher know that no way was I going to mess up in my exams because of all the aggro at home.

Suggested re-write: I told my teacher that under no circumstances would I do badly in my exams because of all the trouble at home.

● **DO NOT USE YOURSELF AS AN AUTHORITY FOR A GENERAL STATEMENT**
Do not write: I think pollution is increasing dangerously and that there should be strict laws controlling it.
Suggested re-write: There is widespread consensus that pollution is out of hand and that new laws and their enforcement are now needed to bring it under control.

● **TAKE CARE IN USING METAPHORS**
Do not write: It was raining cats and dogs and we were not within shouting distance of shelter.
Suggested re-write: It was raining very heavily and there was no shelter in sight.

● **AVOID REPETITION AND PADDING**
Do not write: The postman rang the bell and when I opened the door he handed me a parcel. I noticed immediately that the parcel was for Mrs O'Brien. Mrs O'Brien lives two doors up from us. Mrs O'Brien is our neighbour.
Suggested re-write: The postman rang the bell and when I opened the door he handed me a parcel. I noticed it was addressed to Mrs O'Brien, our neighbour, who lives two doors up the road from us.

● **AVOID IRRELEVANCE (NOT KEEPING TO THE TOPIC)**
Stay with the topic you have chosen to write about. If you are asked to write about the *causes* of crime, do not write about crime *in general*.

● **DISPLAY YOUR LITERACY SKILLS**
Use capital letters, punctuation marks, paragraphs, correct spelling. In referring to titles of books, use inverted commas, especially if the title of a book is the name of a character in the book. For example: 'Hamlet' (inverted commas to signify the play) but Hamlet (without inverted commas, to signify the character).

When using dialogue, indent as for a new paragraph when a different character speaks in the dialogue.

For example:

'Did you see that film last night?' John asked.

'Yes. It was really interesting,' Mary replied. 'But I saw it before and I thought it was great then.'

'I wouldn't mind seeing it again myself,' John said.

UNPUNCTUATED AND NOT PARAGRAPHED:

the most exciting thing about computers is that they go wrong a lot and if they do not break down on their own we help them do so our uniquely human ability to subdue technology which according to the science fiction writers is gearing up to ravage our intelligence is on constant and open display of all the bits and pieces connected to computers floppy disks case us the most pain somebody plonks a computer in front of you gives you instructions on how to boot the machine by sticking brown or black cardboard squares into it but nobody bothers to explain that the disks are actually supersensitive magnetic slivers INSIDE the cardboard and have to be treated with the sort of care normally reserved for ancient manuscripts it is no wonder then that many people regard disks as little more than pieces of cardboard and use them as coffee mats stick them to notice boards or staple them to reports

PUNCTUATED AND PARAGRAPHED:

The most exciting thing about computers is that they go wrong a lot. And if they do not break down on their own, we help them to do so. Our uniquely human ability to subdue technology — which according to the science fiction writers is gearing up to ravage our intelligence — is on constant and open display.

Of all the bits and pieces connected to computers, floppy disks cause us the most pain. Somebody plonks a computer in front of you, gives you instructions on how to 'boot' the machine by sticking brown or black cardboard squares into it, but nobody bothers to explain that the disks are actually supersensitive magnetic slivers INSIDE the cardboard and have to be treated with the sort of care normally reserved for ancient manuscripts. It is no wonder then that many people regard disks as little more than pieces of cardboard and use them as coffee mats, stick them to notice boards, or staple them to reports.

● QUESTIONS

Punctuate and paragraph the following passages:

1.

the round window of my chamber looked out upon the prison yard it was very high from the ground but by placing the table against the wall and mounting upon it i could see everything that was going on in the court yard beneath the window under the slope of the roof the doves had built themselves a nest and when i set about looking out of my window down in the court below they began cooing above my head i had lots of time to make the acquaintance of the inhabitants of the prison yard from my coign of vantage and i knew already that the merriest member of that grim and grey population went by the name of Zazubrina he was a square set stout little fellow with a ruddy face and a high forehead from beneath which his large bright lively eyes sparkled incessantly his cap he wore at the back of his head his ears stuck out on both sides of his shaven head as if in joke he never fastened the strings of his shirt collar he never buttoned his vest and every movement of his muscles gave you to understand that he was a merry soul and a pronounced enemy of anger and sadness

2.

the division of the plays into acts and scenes was not made by shakespeare but later by his editors nevertheless it was not forced on them they lend themselves to it easily by virtue of their inward structure the original texts printed without break nevertheless stood out by a rigour of construction and development which is rare in our time this applies particularly to the thematic development usually contained in the middle of the drama that is to say in the third and some part of the second and fourth acts this section is as it were the box which holds the mainspring of the mechanism at the beginning and conclusion of his play shakespeare freely improvises the details and with as light a heart disposes of the loose ends the swiftly changing scenes are full of life they are drawn from nature with the utmost freedom and with a staggering wealth of imagination

● Do not use sweeping statements

Do not write: No one really cares about anyone anymore.

Suggested re-write: Some people have little care for others.

● ARGUMENT TOPICS

1. What it takes to be a leader.

2. Isn't it time to limit the use of private cars?

3. Science and technology have made our lives more enjoyable.

4. The place of religion in modern society.

5. What makes a good youth club?

6. The beauty and ugliness of life.

7. Famine in a world of plenty.

8. 'Modern music is little more than deafening noise.' Debate or discuss.

9. 'Patriotism has no place in the modern world.' Debate or discuss.

10. The advantages and disadvantages of emigration.

11. City life — country life: the problems are the same.

12. 'The fun has gone out of sport.' Debate or discuss.

13. 'The world has changed for the worse.' Debate or discuss.

14. A letter to God.

15. The value of sport.

16. 'Everything is disposable.' Debate or discuss.

17. 'Censorship is a necessary evil.' Debate or discuss.

18. School — a waste of time!

19. 'Young people today have it far too easy.' Debate or discuss.

20. 'Money is the most important thing in life.' Debate or discuss.

21. Youth is wasted on the young.

22. Boys and girls should have the same education.

23. The young — slaves of fads and fashions.

24. The unemployment problem.

25. The value of the visual arts.

26. People must learn from the experiences of others.

27. Your view of women's liberation.

28. Preserving our heritage is a luxury we cannot afford.

29.   Drug abuse.

30.   Reafforestation.

31.   The teenage cultural scene — worthless and transient.

32.   The inventiveness of the human mind — our glory or doom?

33.   What future for 'The Third World'?

34.   An open letter to the Minister for Education.

35.   Is it time for male liberation now?

36.   What place for literature in the television age?

37.   Violence in everyday life.

38.   Man's inhumanity to man.

39.   Art in everyday life.

40.   After the Holocaust.

41.   'School has failed us.' Debate or discuss.

42.   The ideal school.

43.   Graffiti — art or vandalism?

44.   Europe — long live the difference!

45.   'Religion is a notable force for good in the world.' Debate or discuss.

46.   Nature's disregard for human beings.

47.   This great stage of fools.

48.   The importance of drama.

49.   Breaking barriers.

50.   Modern snobbery.

51.   The pressures to conform.

52.   Telling lies — a real necessity.

53.   The ills of modern society.

54.   Technology — friend or foe?

55.   'Discrimination is non-existent in modern Ireland.' Debate or discuss.

56.   Neither a borrower nor a lender be.

57. Soap operas — suds or something more important?

58. Justice — the forgotten virtue?

59. There is no real way to control crime. Like poverty, it has always been with us.

60. Human beings never learn from their mistakes.

61. My country right or wrong.

62. Life is a tragedy to those who feel; a comedy to those who think.

63. This world of ours is a human zoo.

64. Making an impression.

65. The 'instant' mentality of modern life.

66. Why read poetry?

67. The age of chivalry is dead … and it's just as well!

68. A woman's place is in the home.

69. The world owes me a living.

70. Prisons — the wrong answer.

71. Violence in sport.

72. The lessons of history.

73. The future of religion.

74. After school — what then?

75. As a reader you are free.

76. Freedom of expression — a right or a privilege?

77. Human beings are more the victims than the conquerors of their environment.

78. Science without conscience will be the ruin of the human race.

79. The world does not progress — it merely changes.

80. The computer — friend or foe?

CRITICISING AN ARGUMENTATIVE PASSAGE

What you are asked for:

Comprehension: How well do you understand the passage? How well can you follow the argument? This tests your vocabulary, your general knowledge (references or allusions), your reasoning ability (logic, etc.).

Analysis: This is a test of your ability to assess the effectiveness of the argument, the use the writer makes of evidence, etc. How does the writer develop the argument? How reliable is the evidence used?

JUDGEMENT

You are being asked to judge how effectively the writer has achieved his or her purpose in writing the passage. Do you agree or disagree with the writer's views? Can you give reasons for your own opinions?

THE EFFECTIVENESS OF THE PASSAGE

How well does the writer achieve his or her intention(s)? What techniques of language, such as the use of metaphors, simile, emotive language, deductive and inductive arguments, does the writer employ?

Style: This involves tone, viewpoint and personality. What is the writer's attitude towards the reader and towards the subject matter? Humorous? Serious? Cynical? What is the writer's view of the world? What kind of values do you think the writer holds? Are there any peculiarities in the writer's use of language that convey a sense of personality?

AN ARGUMENTATIVE ESSAY

❮ BOXING*

[Having read the following essay, it will be evident that the writer is proposing that boxing as it is should be banned.]

'Boxing is just showbusiness with blood.' — Frank Bruno, quoted in *The Guardian*, London, Nov. 19, 1991.

Gerald McClellan suffered a serious brain injury last Saturday night. It is likely he will survive. It is also very likely that he will have suffered such serious and permanent damage to his brain that he will never be the same again.

---

* By Steven Young, FRCS, consultant neurosurgeon. From *The Irish Times*, March 4, 1995.

Much will depend on which part of the brain was damaged by the blood clot and whether the secondary brain swelling, that always results from such an injury, can be controlled.

[The issue: The damage inflicted in boxing would justify banning the 'sport'.]

To those who have made a study of boxing injuries, there was nothing surprising about the tragedy: many boxers have died or been seriously injured in the ring. What does surprise is the continuing widespread support for a sport in which victory is determined by the amount of brain damage done to the opponent.

[Counter-arguing the 'glamour' of a knockout.]

A 'knockout' is nothing more or less than concussion severe enough to render a man comatose. When a gloved fist strikes the chin or temple, the brain is accelerated within the skull, causing shearing of long nerve tracts. The force of impact can be considerable: a laboratory experiment revealed that Frank Bruno's punches were equivalent to a blow to the human head of 0.63 tonnes. **[Inductive reasoning.]**

[The inadequacy of the 'safety precautions' argument.]

In McClellan's case, it's likely that an uppercut to the chin resulted in tearing of blood vessels either in the brain or on its surface. He was obviously being well attended by ringside doctors, but within a few minutes the damage to the brain would have been done. Surgery could do no more than remove blood and damaged tissue for, as yet, no way has been found to repair damaged brain.

[The use of medical or scientific evidence to advance the argument against boxing.]

The dramatic events of last Saturday attracted widespread media attention. What needs to be emphasised is that brain damage gradually develops in most boxers — it is just a question of time. Post-mortems reveal that as many as 80 per cent of men who have regularly boxed, whether in a professional or amateur capacity, have signs of brain damage. **[Inductive reasoning.]**

Magnetic resonance scanning, a very sensitive test of brain injury, would appear to verify this worrying condition in living boxers. The effects of repeated trauma to the brain are not obvious in most young boxers, but there is evidence that intellectual deterioration will be detected in many following psychological tests.

[Further use of scientific evidence to advance the argument against boxing.]
Dementia occurring long after retirement from boxing is so well recognised that it has been given its own name — *dementia pugilistica*, which is indistinguishable from Alzheimer's disease. Research has shown that the severity of the condition correlates with the length of a boxer's career and the number of bouts.

Parkinson's disease, another consequence of boxing — well-known because of the way in which it has afflicted Muhammad Ali — is also due to repetitive brain damage. **[Inductive reasoning.]**

[Counter-argument against the 'safety precautions' argument.]
The American and British medical associations have now, formally, called for a ban on boxing. Boxing authorities, in response, have taken steps to make the sport safer. Brain scans are now the norm before and after bouts, and referees are expected to intervene if a fighter seems to be taking too much punishment.

It is usual to have experienced doctors in attendance at both professional and amateur fights. However, it is doubtful whether conventional CT scans are of value in predicting brain damage, and there are limitations — all too obvious last Saturday night — as to what any doctor can do when faced with a serious brain injury at the ringside. Compulsory head gear, avoidance of blows to the head and improved boxing ring floors would all help to reduce the chance of injury.

[Summary of essay: The writer's opinion expressed in this last sentence has considerable persuasive authority because we know that he has the expert knowledge of a neurosurgeon.]
The stark reality, however, is that if we want to continue with this kind of entertainment, the price is always going to be exceptionally high.

QUESTIONS

1. What arguments does the writer bring against the sport of boxing? How effective do you think these arguments are?

2. What indications do you find throughout this article that it is not simply a neutral piece of writing by a medical expert? In your answer, make specific references to the text.

3. How would you describe the tone of this article? Do you think the tone of the piece contributes in some way to the writer's case?

4. Write a reply to this article taking the side of supporters of boxing as a sport.

5. Do you think the writer makes any use of emotive language to advance his argument? Give examples.

ANOTHER ARGUMENTATIVE ESSAY

A FUTURE FOR READING by GEORGE STEINER*

[The first two paragraphs raise the issue of the topic: The future of reading literature. Note the use of statistics in raising the topic.]

It is hardly necessary for me to cite all the evidence of the depressing state of literacy. These figures from the Department of Education are sufficient: 27 million Americans cannot read at all, and a further 35 million read at a level that is less than sufficient to survive in our society.

But my own worry is less that of the overwhelming problem of elemental literacy than it is of the slightly more luxurious problem of the decline in the skills even of the middle-class reader, of his unwillingness to afford those spaces of silence, those luxuries of domesticity and time and concentration, that surround the image of the classic act of reading. It has been suggested that almost 80 per cent of America's *literate*, educated teenagers can no longer read without an attendant noise (music) in the background or a television screen flickering at the corner of their field of perception. We know very little about the cortex and how it deals with simultaneous conflicting input, but every common-sense hunch suggests we should be profoundly alarmed. This breach of concentration, silence,

---

*Part of the R.B. Bowker Memorial Lecture give by the critic George Steiner in 1985. Later published in *Publishers Weekly*.

solitude goes to the very heart of our notion of literacy; this new form of part-reading, of part-perception against background distraction, renders impossible certain essential acts of apprehension and concentration, let alone that most important tribute any human being can pay to a poem or a piece of prose he or she really loves, which is to *learn it by heart*. Not by brain, by heart; the expression is vital.

[How the issue raised will be dealt with.]
Under these circumstances, the question of what future there is for the arts of reading is a real one. Ahead of us lie technical, psychic, and social transformations probably much more dramatic than those brought about by Gutenberg. The Gutenberg revolution, as we know it, took a long time; its effects are still being debated. The information revolution will touch every facet of composition, publication, distribution, and reading. No one in the book industry can say with any confidence what will happen to the book as we've known it.

[What the writer means by 'reading'.]
It now looks as if the arts of reading will fall into three distinct categories. The first will continue to be the vast, amorphous mass of reading for distraction, for momentary entertainment — the airport book. I suspect that this kind of reading will more and more involve not cheap paperbacks but cable transmissions to home-screens. You will select the book you wish, the speed at which you wish the pages to be turned. Some texts will be read to the viewer by a professional reader. Whether or not the text will appear on the screen as it is being read is an open question.

The second kind of reading will be for information — what De Quincey called 'the literature of knowledge', to distinguish it from fiction, poetry, and drama, which he called 'the literature of power'. The means to acquire the literature of knowledge — the micro circuit, the silicon chip, the laser disc — will alter our habits beyond anything we can now conceive. 'The Library of Babel', the library of all possible libraries that Borges imagined in his fable, will be literally and concretely accessible for personal and institutional use. We will be able to summon it up on a screen, and here the possibility of a basic change in the structures of attention and understanding is almost incommensurable.

What about reading in the old, private, silent sense? This may become as specialised a skill and avocation as it was in the scriptoria and libraries of monasteries during the so-called Dark Ages. We now know these were in fact key ages, radiant in their patience, radiant in their sense of what had to be copied and preserved. Private libraries may once again become as notable and rare as they were when Erasmus and Montaigne were famous for theirs. The habit of furnishing a room, a large room, possibly, with shelves and filling them with books, not paperbacks but bound books, the attempt to collect the complete editions of an author (itself a very special concept) as well as the first editions, not necessarily the rare books of the Morgan Library but the first editions of a modern author, with the hope of owning everything by a writer — good, bad, or indifferent — whom one loves; the ability — above all, the wish — to attend to a demanding text, to master the grammar, the arts of memory, the tactics of repose and concentration that great books demand — these may once more become the practices of an élite, of a mandarinate of silence.

[The threat to reading as the writer understands 'reading'.]

Such a mandarinate, such an élite of book men and book women, will not have the power, the political reach, or the prestige that it had during the Renaissance and the Enlightenment, and almost to the end of the Victorian age. That power almost inevitably will belong to the alliterate. It will belong to the numerate. It will belong increasingly to those who, while technically almost unable to read a serious book and mostly unwilling to do so, can in preadolescence produce software of great delicacy, logical power, and conceptual depth. The power relations are shifting to them, to men and women who, having freed themselves from the heavy burden of actual alphabetic literacy and its constant referential habits, from the fact that almost all great literature refers to other great literature, are *creators* — nonreaders, but creators of a new kind.

[Summary of argument for reading.]

Returning home one night, Erasmus is said to have seen a torn piece of print besmirched in the mud. As he bent to pick it up, he uttered a cry of joy, overcome by the wonder of the book, by the sheer miracle of what lies behind picking up such a message. Today, in a vast traffic jam on a highway or in a Manhattan grid, we can insert a cassette of the *Missa Solemnis* into a tape deck. We can, via paperbacks and soon cable television, demand, command, and compel the world's greatest, most exigent, most tragic or delightful literature to be served up for us, packaged and cellophaned for immediacy. These are great luxuries. But it is not certain that they really help the constant, renewed miracle that is the encounter with a book.

QUESTIONS

1. What do you think is the writer's main intention in writing this essay? Where do you find this intention most explicitly stated?

2. Analyse the writer's use of allusions or references to support his arguments. Give examples and discuss their effectiveness.

3. What arguments does the writer use to support his view of the future of reading? How convincing do you find these arguments?

4. The writer has a special understanding of reading which he divides into three categories. Describe these categories.

5. Do you think the writer's pessimistic view of the future of reading is justified? Give reasons for your answer.

6. How would you describe the tone of this essay in respect of the writer's attitude towards his subject and towards his readers? Illustrate your comments with references to the text.

ONE MORE ARGUMENTATIVE ESSAY

SOAPS, CYNICISM, AND MIND CONTROL by ELIZABETH JANEWAY*

[Introducing the topic by asking questions.]

What does the powerful teaching tool of television have to say to its viewers about desirable attitudes toward life and its problems? And what does the Media Establishment assume that *we* assume about the way this world functions? With these questions, I approached soap operas and evening series — programmes that claim to present ordinary existence, though heightened for drama and catering to everyone's curiosity about how the other half lives.

---

*Ms magazine, Jan. 1985

[The notion of 'randomness' as a 'handle' for the topic.]

In between commercial breaks, I noted a deeply disturbing factor in so many of the dramas: the lack of any sense of process, of the eternal truth that events have consequences, and that people can and do influence what happens to them and to others. What I saw instead was a consistent, insistent demonstration of *randomness*, a statement that life is unpredictable and out of control. With rare exceptions what happens on-screen suggests that no one can trust her or his judgment and (other side of the same coin) that no one, friend, kin, or lover, is really trustworthy.

[Development of the notion of 'randomness'.]

We may identify with the actors because we all face unpredictable events, but we get no clues to coping with them. No one seems talented at solving the puzzles of life: even J R Ewing was shot. Nobody shows us how to decide on the fidelity of kin and associates, no love is certain. Let a wedding date be set and you can be pretty sure the ceremony won't come off. Report a death and expect the corpse to show up in a future segment fleeing a crime, amnesiac, or as a survivor of a 'fatal' plane crash. Says one of a pair of embracing lovers: 'I don't know anything about you.' Par for the course. Later in the same segment (of 'Another World') a young woman tells a young man she doesn't love him. But wait a minute! She has been hypnotised, it seems, in a programme I missed, and here she is on tape declaring she *does* love him to the hypnotist. Not only don't we/they know anything about the others in their lives, they/we don't understand ourselves either. The Guiding Lights we seek are shrouded in fog.

[The controlling notion of 'predictability.]

Now drama, and indeed fiction as a whole, has always aimed at surprising its audiences. But those surprises end by showing us something we hadn't known, some truth, about existence. It may be a tragic truth, but tragedy can strengthen us to face the future because it explains and illustrates the processes that lead to defeat instead of victory. And knowledge is power. Even when it tells us some things can't be changed, it differentiates inevitability from potentiality; and moreover, it gives us a chance to plan our own responses: we can't change the weather, but we can take an umbrella when we go out. Our intervention is shown to be possible. Beginning with childhood fables and fairy tales, such stories bring us useful messages about the workings of the real world and what human beings can do to influence it.

That's not what TV programmes say. The people on the screen are adrift in a world of happenstance, and the messages warn that no action will do any good.

[Arguments against 'randomness'.]

Certainly there's a lot of randomness in the world. Stable unchanging small-town life is fading from the American scene and close ties to extended families are rare. Most of us meet a lot of strangers from unfamiliar backgrounds. Women who have moved into formerly all-male preserves have had to learn or invent patterns of relationships as well as new processes of doing things. These women have begun to take risks and forget old lessons in helplessness. But daily there appears on the screen counsel that the world is unpredictable, that one can't hope to plan or gain control of events. Moreover when we see the rare realistic portrayal of work-life (where competence, daring, and imagination may be rewarded), attention is concentrated on the personal. Intimate relationships are chancy and dangerous, comes the word, but they're the only things that matter.

Randomness, like guilt, is a powerful tool for social control. Survivors of the Holocaust and refugees from Stalin's 'Gulag Archipelago' record how personality was deliberately broken down by those in control disrupting their prisoners' normal expectations. Guards separated consequences from action and thus persuaded prisoners that it was hopeless for them to plan a particular behaviour, hopeless for them to imagine a future. Survival became a matter of utter chance. Inmates of the camps were thus reduced to subhuman, mindless robots who moved as they were told to.

Today in El Salvador (and who can say how many other places?), terror activates the randomness of danger. No one knows where the death squads will strike next, and therefore people can't take any reasonable action and expect to ensure greater safety. *Time* magazine quotes an expert on Central America in a recent issue: 'Anybody can be killed with virtual impunity. You do not want to investigate because you might find out, and finding out can itself be fatal.'

But it's not only in extreme situations that randomness can be used to promote self-policing. If the powerful can divide the majority of ordinary folk into disconnected, self-protecting individuals, they need not fear organised resistance. And when television suggests to a woman that even her friends had better not be trusted, it is denying comradeship, sisterhood — and joint action.

[Summary of the argument.]

I don't suggest that this is a conscious media conspiracy intended to keep women and other groups in their subordinate places. *It doesn't need to be.* Standard practice and the mythic ideology that enforces it have always played up individual effort as a way of establishing one's value and one's deserts. For instance, the Supreme Court has underlined that message by limiting affirmative action remedies that can be awarded to a group or class. Legal recourse must now be sought by *individuals* rather than on a group basis. When the media repeats this message, it need only appeal to what we've often heard before: success means learning the rules and following them. Don't trust your colleagues. The big world of action is both dangerous and mysterious, you'll never really understand it. Stay out of it, sit still, don't try.

Will we follow that message more than two generations after women won the ballot? Let us refuse the posture of the powerless. People who have begun to feel strong don't have to accept victimisation.

● QUESTIONS

1. Sum up the writer's main arguments against television soaps.

2. Analyse the writer's idea of 'randomness' which she explains in the first two paragraphs.

3. Show how the writer develops the charge of 'randomness' against soaps.

4. What are the dangers which the writer sees in her concept of 'randomness'? How convincing do you find her presentation of these dangers?

5. Do you find the essay make a persuasive case against soaps? Give reasons for your answer.

6. Taking account of the writer's attack on soaps, write an essay in their defence.

7. Would you agree that this essay is about more than soaps? What else do you think it might be about?

THE LANGUAGE OF NARRATIVE: PERSONAL WRITING

Narrative writing when not applied to straightforward fiction can be conveniently described as 'The Language of Personality'. It is a certain kind of writing or genre in which the *personality* of the writer takes precedence over other factors such as subject matter, narrative form, theme, etc. Its primary function is entertainment of the reader by the writer *as himself or herself*, although the writer may do this indirectly by using invented characters. This writing is not fiction proper but a self-conscious use of fictional means to make what the writer has to say more interesting or more amusing.

Personal writing is not, for its own sake, informational, argumentative or narrative, though it may exploit the techniques of all these forms of writing. It is writing that expresses a personal style, that communicates a sense of a writer's individual personality. It is usually a form of narrative writing.

Nowadays the personal essay is usually to be found as 'Viewpoint' or 'Opinion' columns in newspapers and magazines.

ELEMENTS OF NARRATIVE WRITING

Note: It is by putting one's own personal stamp on the following elements that a personal style is created.

● **Diction or vocabulary**
● **Idioms**
● **Sentence structure**
● **Similes and metaphors**
● **Choice of subject matter**
● **Treatment of subject matter**

- Theme
- Attitude of the writer towards the reader
- Nature and range of references or allusions

DICTION OR VOCABULARY

Does the writer have a preference for simple everyday words?

Does the writer enjoy using long and unusual words?

Does the writer use slang or street expressions?

Is the writer very precise in the use of words?

Is the writer's vocabulary contemporary?

Does the writer use archaic (old-fashioned) words to achieve certain effects?

Is the writer's vocabulary historical? Is it characteristic of a certain period of writing such as the eighteenth or nineteenth century?

EXERCISES

Comment on the diction of the following passages:

1.

About the time I turned 16, my folks began to wonder why I didn't stay home any more. I always had an excuse for them, but what I didn't say was that I had found my freedom and I was getting out.

I went through four years of high school in semi-rural Alabama and became active in clubs and sports; I made a lot of friends and became a regular guy, if you know what I mean. But one thing was irregular about me: I managed those four years without ever having a friend visit at my home.

I was ashamed of where I lived. I had been ashamed for as long as I had been conscious of class.

2.

On my right hand there were lines of fishing stakes resembling a mysterious system of half-submerged bamboo fences, incomprehensible in its division of the domain of tropical fishes, and crazy of aspect as if abandoned forever by some nomad tribe now gone to the other end of the ocean; for there was no sign of human habitation as far as the eye could reach. To the left a group of barren islets, suggesting ruins set in a blue sea that itself looked solid, so still and stable did it lie below my feet; even the track of light from the westering sun shone smoothly, without that animated glitter which tells of an imperceptible ripple.

3.

There was here a lady who had received an education of nine months in London, and this gave her pretensions to taste, which rendered her the indisputable mistress of the ceremonies wherever she came. She was informed of my merits; everybody praised me, yet she refused at first going to see me perform. She could not conceive, she said, anything but stuff from a stroller; talked something in praise of Garrick, and amazed the ladies with her skill in enunciations, tones, and cadences.

4.

My Aunt Jack, who was my father's aunt as well as mine, sometimes came down from where she lived, up near the Basin, where the water came from before they started getting it from Wicklow. My Aunt Jack said it was much better water, at that. Miss McCann said she ought to be a good judge. For Aunt Jack was funny. She didn't drink porter or malt, or take snuff, and my father said she never thought much about men, either. She was also very strict about washing yourself very often. My grandmother took a bath every year, whether she was dirty or not, but she was in no way bigoted in the washing line in between times.

IDIOMS

An idiom is an expression peculiar to a certain language. It does not mean what it says literally. For example: 'To make hay while the sun shines' has nothing to do with haymaking but means 'to take full advantage of a good opportunity'. Good idioms add colour and vividness to writing. Poor idioms — those exhausted through over-use — are a dead weight.

Some common idioms:
to beggar description: to defy description
to hang back: to linger

to brazen out: to defend shamelessly

to have one's head in the clouds: to be unaware of everyday realities

a cock-and-bull story: an incredible story

to curry favour: to try to be popular

to be down in the dumps: to be depressed

to fight shy of: to keep clear of

the ins and outs: the details

to be on one's last legs: to be almost exhausted

to make off with: to run away with or steal

a makeshift: something temporary

down in the mouth: glum or depressed

at a pinch: in an emergency

to take a rise out of someone: to make fun of someone

to give the cold shoulder to: to snub

SENTENCE STRUCTURE

Does the writer use simple sentences with few modifiers or qualifiers, expressing a rather simple black-or-white view of things?

Is this use of simple sentences natural or deliberately contrived?

Does the writer use complex sentences filled with qualifying clauses, expressing a sophisticated and complicated way of looking at the world?

Does the writer imitate the complex sentence-structures of the past?

Comment briefly on the use of sentence structure in the following passages:

1. And this is how I see the East. I have seen its secret places and have looked into its very soul; but now I see it always from a small boat, a high outline of mountains, blue and far in the morning; like faint mist at noon; a jagged wall of purple at sunset. I have the feel of the oar in my hand, the vision of a scorching blue sea in my eyes.

2. As Al saw it, there was only one solution. He had to get rid of the dog without Betty or the kids finding out about it. At night. It would have to be done at night. He would simply drive Suzy — well, someplace, later he'd decide where — open the door, push her out, drive away. The sooner the better. He felt relieved making the decision. Any action was better than no action at all, he was becoming convinced.

SIMILIES AND METAPHORS

(A simile and a metaphor are both comparisons; the simile is introduced by the word 'like' or 'as', the metaphor is not.)

Does the writer make use of many similes and metaphors?

Are these fresh and effective or hackneyed and worn-out?

What do they tell the reader about the writer's interest and way of seeing things?

EXERCISES

Match these well-tried metaphors with their meanings which follow:

Metaphors:

1. birds of a feather
2. a bone of contention
3. to burn one's bridges
4. to bury the hatchet
5. to put one's cards on the table
6. to see which way the cat jumps
7. to let the cat out of the bag
8. to go under false colours
9. on the horns of a dilemma
10. a dog in a manger
11. to feather one's nest
12. to put the fat in the fire
13. a fish out of water
14. the fly in the ointment
15. a fair-weather friend
16. to fall between two stools
17. to grease someone's palm
18. the lion's share
19. to wear one's heart on one's sleeve
20. to keep one's head above water

Meanings:

1. to bribe someone
2. the biggest share
3. something out of its proper place
4. to try to do two things and fail at both
5. to wait and see how things turn out
6. the one thing wrong with something
7. to just about manage
8. to look after one's own interests
9. people of the same sort or views
10. to make it impossible to go back
11. to be open and frank
12. to reveal a secret
13. to make peace
14. an issue of dispute or argument
15. someone who does not want anyone else to enjoy what he or she cannot
16. to pretend to be what someone or something is not
17. to show one's emotions too easily or unnecessarily
18. to have to choose between two equally unpleasant options
19. a friend who is only a friend in good times
20. to cause a great upset by revealing a secret

MIXED METAPHORS

As the phrase indicates, mixed metaphors are metaphors that do not naturally or logically go together. They occur because those who use them are no longer aware of their metaphoric value and are only thinking of what they mean as statement. They usually occur when the metaphors are exhausted through over-use and have lost their visual or figurative impact.

EXAMPLES

- He was the black sheep of the family, a rolling stone.
  = He was the disreputable member of the family who never stayed long in any one place.

- He ruled the roost although he was a snake in the grass.
  = He was domineering although he was sly.

- She was born with a silver spoon in her mouth and was forever blowing her own trumpet.
  = She was born into wealth and was forever boasting about herself.

- He is a wolf in sheep's clothing pretending to pour oil on troubled waters.
  = He concealed his viciousness under the guise of meekness, pretending he was a peacemaker.

- She tried to be a new broom but only managed to put a nail in her own coffin.
  = She tried to clean up the situation but ended up doing herself harm.

EXERCISES

Invent *five* examples of mixed metaphors and give their meaning as plain statement.

Some hackneyed or worn-out similes to be avoided:

to roar like a lion	wily as a fox
to fight like a bull	light as a feather
as gentle as a lamb	as cool as a cucumber
as strong as an ox	as strong as iron
as green as grass	as hard as stone
to sink like a stone	as sharp as a razor
to cry like a baby	as sweet as honey
to go off like a rocket	as bitter as vinegar
as white as snow	soft as a pillow
slippery as an eel	rare as gold

CHOICE OF SUBJECT MATTER

Is the writer's choice of subject matter in any way characteristic of the writer?

Is the subject matter of the writer what one might expect having read other things by the writer? For example, does the writer characteristically write about working-class life (Roddy Doyle) or about the sea (Joseph Conrad)?

TREATMENT OF SUBJECT MATTER

Is the writer's treatment of the subject matter characteristically humorous, serious, playful, cynical, whimsical, moralising, etc.?

What biases or prejudices does the writer's treatment of the subject matter reveal?

How would you characterise the treatment of subject in the following passage?

I do not consider pigeons birds, in the first place. They are more in the nature of people; people who mooch. Probably my feeling about pigeons arises from the fact that all my life I have lived in rooms where pigeons came rumbling in and out of my window.

THEME

This is the idea, insight or intention which the writer tries to express (see page 36).

ATTITUDE OF THE WRITER TOWARDS THE READER

Does the writer regard the reader as (a) an equal in knowledge and intelligence (b) a potentially sympathetic person (c) an inferior to be made a fool of (d) someone who holds a view the writer wishes to change?

Comment on the writer's attitude towards the reader in the following passage:

I have been misunderstood and wrongly accused so many times that I ought to be able to shrug my shoulders, not merely suffering in silence (for I know that protest is useless) but being indifferent, not suffering at all. Yet every other day or so something happens and I see once more what an ill-fated fellow I am.

NATURE AND RANGE OF REFERENCES OR ALLUSIONS

What indications of his or her education, social class, expert knowledge, are provided by the nature and scope of the writer's references?

What do you learn of the writer of the following passage from the nature of the references?

But this boat was plumb English, codfish nose and mackerel stern. She was, between perpendiculars, twenty-nine and a half-foot. She was, over all, thirty-six foot. She was of cutter rig, she was nine tons — according to the only measurement worth having, and fancy measurements may go to the devil. Four men were happy on board her, five men she could carry, six men quarrelled. She did not sail very close to the wind, for she was of sound tradition and habit, the ninth of her family, and perhaps the last.

Note: The comments in the brackets are intended to assist the student in his or her analysis of this first essay.

◀ SUNDAY by NEIL JORDAN*

[In this first paragraph, the writer immediately personalises the topic by creating a personal sense of atmosphere. He establishes a somewhat

---

*This essay was written by Neil Jordan when he was a Sixth Year student in Saint Paul's College, Raheny, Dublin 5. It won The College President's Essay Prize and was published in the school magazine. It is published with the writer's special permission.

exaggerated and whimsical mood ('collars and ties formalise it') which he will maintain throughout the essay, thus giving the essay the quality of coherence.]

Sunday is a strange day. It is black and white, good and bad at the same time. It elates us during the week, and depresses us when it comes. It is an anti-climax, 'a miserable failure of a holiday', either hot and stuffy or cold and dreary. Rain seems to head for it, wetting the roofs and pavements, darkening the skies. Mist surrounds it, dampening, quenching, thickening, and collars and ties formalise it.

[The writer identifies himself to the reader. He gives his age and shows himself as imaginative.]

Today, at eighteen, I have resigned myself to Sunday. I reserve it for study, for Mass, for eating and sleeping. In the afternoon I scan a bleary book with a bleary eye, and when I tire of that I watch black and white and tortoiseshell cats chase leaves down the lawn. Or, I light a cigarette, lie back, and dream of sailing boats and sealing-wax, of cabbages and kings.

[The writer unfolds his plan of showing what Sunday has meant to him at different stages of his life. By this technique, he can draw on autobiographical material, developing an interesting self-portrait while not departing from the set topic.]

However, this is the defeatist's way of spending Sunday. Sunday afternoon study is for the unimaginative mind, the mind whose sharpness has been dimmed by the Sunday mist and rain. Before I turned to the maturer joy of study, I had many a way of spending it. Each I remember, for my joys then were mainly escapist ones, ones in which the body was preoccupied, but the mind was elsewhere, wandering, thinking, recording the details of the moment.

[For an Irish Catholic youth of the time, Sunday would not have been Sunday without the experience of Mass. Notice how sensitively the experience is presented from the point of view of the child.]

At the age of about three or four, for instance, Sunday was sad and mysterious. Mass was a strange rite, and a heavy and holy atmosphere hung in the church. The bells made me wonder. They would tinkle and everyone would rise, brushing the dust from their knees. The legs looked like so many tree trunks, and the bobbing beads, the muffled coughing, gave the silence a strange solemnity. Mass seemed hours to me then. The hard oak of the kneeling bench cut into my knees, and the tweeds and silks of the dresses brushed into my face. All I could see was a particular pattern, a rose, a sprig of holly or a mass of twining and untwining colour. The trousers were squared or striped, and the tweed could be seen coming through the material in flecks, mixed with specks of dust and clay. These I would examine for what seemed hours. The hands holding prayer books and rosary beads, much bigger than my own, often with rings, or hair on the back running down the fingers. Imagine my amazement when my cousin told me it only lasted thirty minutes.

Of the strange goings on at the altar I knew nothing. It mystified and frightened me, troubled my mind, and yet I would steal biscuits just the same, if I got the chance.

Soon afterwards dinner came, with roast beef and slurping gravy and potatoes, bigger than my fist. I never could get through my dinner, and it usually ended up a sticky mess upon the plate, with my father coaxing me to eat it, my mother bending over me and wrinkling her forehead and nose, telling me how cowboys ate potatoes, to make them big and strong. When that was over, my father would put on a record, often, which he called 'The Hunt'. And we, my brother and I, would jump over the big couch, whooping and yelping, he the fox and I the hunter. I afterwards discovered that it was called 'Charge of the Light Brigade' and was very disappointed.

[The writer chooses to write about a visit to the Museum as typical of his time in Dublin. This broadens the appeal of his essay by allowing many readers to identify with him.]

Or, sometimes we would pile into the old rusty car and go to the Museum. This was a pleasure, especially reserved for Sunday afternoons, and often a dubious one. For it was a cold, although an interesting place, with the wind piping bleakly over the flagstones and through the railings of Merrion Square.

A place of wonders, the Museum was. In one building there were spears and grenades and frightening witch masks from Africa. Curved knives, with carvings twisting and twining down the blades, and rows of rifles. In the other building there were birds and eggs and animals in glass cages. Huge eggs, bigger than a sparrow's or blackbird's, the size of which I had never seen. The greatest wonder, however, was a monster (a dinosaur, they called it), a monstrous mass of bones, reaching to the ceiling, into which I could have fitted about seventy times.

When we changed house to Clontarf, my Sundays changed too. Now I had friends, to be bored or happy with. The collar and tie of Sunday would no longer stifle us, but we would sally forth into Saint Anne's, each one a little Robin Hood, ready to climb the highest tree or defeat the greatest enemy. Makeshift bows of ash and kitchen twine would thicken the air with imaginary arrows. Guns and wooden swords would kill the enemy like flies, every wounded man groaning in terrible agony until the game ended. There were trees to be climbed and branches to be broken, nests to be searched for, and Sunday took on a much more delightful aspect.

[The changing pattern of Sunday reflects the writer's own development into adolescence.]

Needless to say, Mass now had lost much of its interest, as I both knew what happened at the altar and could see beyond the prayer-bench. It was time for even more interesting things, however. For I grew old enough to know of cigarettes and girls, and how to grease my hair and wear a pointed shoe. I would pull a cigarette, give a catcall as well as the rest of my friends. My Sunday afternoons were spent at the pictures, peering over the heads of many, through the smoke, to the flickering screen. Or, I went down to the local shop and chewed Tayto crisps and chewing-gum for the day. More often, we would visit the hockey field across the way, and idly kick a ball — with an eye on the girls. Each one trying to outdo the other in daring, we would give an odd whoop or sheepish whistle. Skiting, swishing skirts, tittering laughter, bangs of hockey sticks, cigarettes slightly sickening and long pants — these were not enjoyments but necessities, necessary for conformity, and woe betide him who didn't conform!

[The essay is nicely brought to an end as the writer anticipates what the pattern of his Sundays will be when he enters the next stage of his development: early adulthood.]

And with them Sunday began to bore. It had always been sad, but now it was frustrating. The mist and rain began to appear. Or, rather, my eye began to notice them above the sun and blue sky. When the sun appeared it seemed to make me sweat, rather than to warm me. When the rain came, it wet me more severely than usual. I began to notice Sunday's wetness rather than Sunday's dryness and mirth. Slow smoke rising eternally, silhouetted with grey roofs and television aerials against the muddy sky. The television, blinking, droning, unending, always waiting to be watched. These are Sunday scenes. They are grey, lifeless and uninteresting. Perhaps next year's Sundays will show a different pattern. Or those when I'm twenty one or twenty two. Perhaps I'll lose my legs, become a Mohammedan, kill my great-grandfather, and change the nature of Sunday. Only time will tell.

● QUESTIONS

1. How would you describe the writer's treatment of the subject matter? Humorous? Serious? Playful? Illustrate your comments with references to the text.

2. What impression of the writer's personality does the essay convey? Refer to the writer's use of specific details of his life.

3. How does the changing pattern of his Sundays reflect the writer's own development into adolescence?

4. Comment on the writer's use of similes and metaphors. Illustrate your comments with specific examples.

5. How well structured do you think this essay is as a piece of personal writing?

6. Would you agree that the appeal of this essay is to be found in the writer's treatment of his subject matter rather than in the intrinsic interest of the subject itself?

◀ THE LAW'S DECAY by PATRICK KAVANAGH*

I took part in a discussion in a barley field one evening about the decline in going to law with your neighbour. I have mentioned this matter before but a second run will do no harm. 'Yez have me disgraced,' said the old Parish Priest to a group of his parishioners whom he met at the station on their way home after a day's swearing.

Some of these swearers were, I believe, top class and worthy to be mentioned with those found in Somerville and Ross.

I know that my own people spent many happy hours going to law with our neighbours over a right o' way to a well. The first bout went against us and the

---

* from *Collected Pruse* by Patrick Kavanagh (MacGibbon & Kee, London, 1967)

winners were loudly grigged: 'We had our Blessed Lady and Saint Patrick on our side.'

We appealed to the higher court and this time our saints won.

Nowadays, if you aren't careful, some fellow will make you a present of a corner over which many a suit was waged. And that's a thing you have to be careful of — being encumbered with property. A year or so ago I got a present of a Dunlopillo bed and a couple of good armchairs and for a few months I was their slave. The wonderful thing is to be able to walk off with your shillelagh under your arm.

Now though I come from a lawbred country, it is a curious fact that until the spring of nineteen fifty-four, I had never been an active participant in law. I have never been to jail either, and so have missed being a famous playwright.

An epic battle was fought in those regions some years ago, in the twenties, I think. A long and very narrow lane prevented Barney Campbell and the Duck Farrell from getting their corn threshed except with the flail. That year they decided to bring in the threshing mill, hit or miss. Like a bulldozing tank the mill went for the narrow lane. In front of the engine was the Pioneer Corps with hacks and shovels widening the lane.

The owners of the land adjoining came into action. Volley after volley of stones poured on to the road wideners. The women of the military tribe kept supplying apronfuls of stones.

I was a youth at the time and I well remember listening to the wild huzzas — like the ancient Irish abusing the enemy by word of mouth, which also helped to keep up morale. This was part of the fight. The gallant engine driver was hit with a splinter of whin stone but he bravely kept his post.

As far as I remember this epic of the lane lasted the best part of three weeks. I often walked that way afterwards and saw the great boulders that had been dug from the sides of the lane. And if you don't believe me, ask Pat Keegan. The railroad got through.

I often wonder who paid the lawyers or were they, too, in it for pleasure. Of course, it isn't just the ordinary man who is mad for law. There was that Foyle's Fisheries case which must have run for a generation.

With some sadness I walk the rural ways these days and see rights o' way that have made many a solicitor's name, gone to ruin. Part of our own well-fought-for rights consisted of two wooden stiles leading over the railway. When the railway was removed this year they also took the stiles.

This morning I met the local D.J. on the bus on his way to work. Things aren't wot they used to be for magistrates!

QUESTIONS

1.   How would you categorise the writer's use of diction? What do we learn about the writer from the kind of vocabulary he uses?

2.   How would you describe the writer's treatment of his topic? Humorous? Serious? Illustrate with references to the text.

3.   What do we learn of the writer's personality from his treatment of the topic?

4.   The writer makes use of mock-heroics in order to create humour. Give examples of this.

5.   What do the references or allusions in the passage tell us about the writer?

6.   Point out some idioms used by the writer and comment on their use and effectiveness.

7.   How would you describe the attitude of the writer towards his readers?

A WELL-PLANNED MURDER by MYLES NA GOPALEEN (FLANN O'BRIEN)*

Years ago when I was living in Islington, a cub reporter in the service of Tay Pay, founder of that modern scourge, the 'gossip column', I had great trouble with my landlord. The man was a vulgar low bowler-hatted plumber who tortured me exquisitely by his vulgarity of dress, talk and aspect. The situation rapidly became Russian. Evenings in the yellow gaslight, myself immersed in a letter to George Harris or painfully compiling my first novel, the gross plumber audibly eating tripe in an armchair behind me. The succession — the crescendo of 'Greek' emotion — irritation — anger — loathing —then hatred. And then the quiet grey thought — I will do this creature in. I will do for him, gorblimey, if I have to swing for it!

It is funny how small things irk far beyond their own intrinsic significance. The way he sucked at his dirty pipe, too lazy or stupid to light it. The trick of never lacing his boots up completely. And his low boasting about his drinking. Forty-eight pints of cider in a Maidenhead inn. Mild and bitter by the gallon. I

---

* from *The Best of Myles* by Myles na Gopaleen (Flann O'Brien). (McGibbon & Kee, London, 1968).

remember retorting savagely on one occasion that I would drink him under the table. Immediately came the challenge to do so. 'Not now,' I remember saying, 'but sooner than you think, my good friend.' That is the way we talked in those days. Possibly it was just then that I first formed my murderous resolution. But I digress.

When I had finally decided to murder this insufferable plumber, I naturally occupied my mind for some days with the mechanics of sudden death. I was familiar with the practice of homicide fashionable in the eighties, and I laid my plans with some care. I took to locking my bedroom so that the paraphernalia of execution could be amassed without arousing the suspicions of the patient. The chopper was duly purchased, together with a spare hatchet in case the plumber's skull should withstand the chopper. I attended a physical culture class to improve my muscles. Alcohol and tobacco were discontinued. I took long walks on Sunday afternoons and slept with the window wide open. But most important of all — remember that I speak of the gaslit eighties — I purchased a large bath and the customary drums of acid.

I was then ready. The precise moment of execution did not matter so much. It would coincide with some supreme extremity of irritation. And it did. One evening re-opening the manuscript of my novel I discovered traces of tripe on the clean copper-plate pages. The wretched plumber had been perusing my private documents. I went upstairs whistling 'The Girl in the Hansom Cab', came down cheerfully with the chopper behind my back, and opened the ruffian's skull from crown to neck with a haymaker of a wallop that nearly broke my own arm. The rest was simple. I carried the body up to my room and put it in the bath of acid. Nothing more remained but to put things in order for my departure next day for a week's holiday with my old parents in Goraghwood, my native place.

When I returned to London, I went up to the bedroom with some curiosity. There was nothing to be seen save the bath of acid. I carried the bath down to the sitting room and got a glass. I filled the glass with what was in the bath, crept in under the table and swallowed the burning liquid. Glass after glass I swallowed till all was gone. It was with grim joy that I accomplished my threat that I would drink this plumber under the table. It was the sort of thing one did at the turn of the century.

QUESTIONS

1. The humour of this piece largely depends on the writer creating a mock-serious atmosphere. How is this achieved by the use of diction and sentence structure?

2. The writer has carefully created the character of the narrator to extract as much humour from the piece as possible. What aspects of this character are exploited to heighten the humour?

3. What details of diction and phrasing clue the reader into the comic nature of the narrative?

4. Would you agree that the success of this piece of comic personal writing depends on the tone at which it is pitched? Remember that tone means the attitude of the writer towards his subject matter and towards the reader.

5. The humour of this piece is dependent on a carefully crafted style. Analyse this style and comment on its appropriateness to the writer's intention.

6. How would you describe the writer's attitude towards his readers?

7. The whole passage may be described as an elaborate pun on the expression 'to drink someone under the table'. Taking a similar expression, outline how you might build a humorous piece on the expression.

◀ THE HABIT OF READING by RICHARD ALDINGTON*

In those days I began to form the habit of reading. Whether you consider that a virtue or a vice is apt to depend on whether you are or are not interested in the book and education trades. It is a habit I have no intention of trying to break. Even if all new books become political and economic propaganda, I shall go on reading old ones, which are more interesting anyway in most cases. I think it was fortunate that my schools paid no attention to 'cultural interests', so that reading was pure fun. I also think I was lucky in having the run of a large general library.

For some time my attention never strayed much beyond a shelf of adventure stories which my father had collected in his boyhood. Christmas and birthdays

---

* from *Life for Life's Sake* by Richard Aldington. (Cassell. London. 1968)

provided me with more recent versions of the gory yarns which for some strange reason are thought suitable for youthful minds.

These I read with great attention and popping eyes, but at last criticism reared its viperous head. Among those bloodthirsty panegyrics of violence was a story about the Wars of the Roses. The name of the author escapes me, but the hero bore the tremendous title of Sir Oswald Athelney. At a certain point in the book Sir Oswald vaulted lightly from his charger at the door of an inn, threw the reins to one of the lower classes conveniently located by the author for that purpose, and strode in with his customary 'Ho! varlets!' That was all right with me, but then Sir Oswald went on to order a beefsteak from the bowing host, adding: 'Let it be brown without and red when I apply my knife.' I paused. Did the scions of chivalry worry about the cooking of steaks? Did they have steaks in those days? A venison pasty or a baron of beef, yes. But a steak! By the simple process of reading the last page first I had learned that Sir Oswald eventually became an earl. I couldn't believe so noble a personage would disgrace himself and fiction by ordering a common beefsteak. Moreover, 'mine knife' didn't sound right either.

I was so worried about this that I put the whole problem to my father, who was most unsympathetic. Without looking up from his own book he said if I didn't like what I was reading I'd better try Scott. That was no good, because I'd already tried Scott and didn't like him. Well, said my father impatiently, try Harrison Ainsworth.

The choice was not altogether happy, and I should have done better to persevere with the far more sensible Scotchman. For months my slumbers were haunted with the Satanic horrors of *The Lancashire Witches*, the revolting descriptions of the great plague in *Old St Paul's*, the frightful tortures in *Guy Fawkes* and *The Tower of London*, and the supernatural terrors of *Auriol*.

Moreover, Ainsworth was a shade too zealous in recording the swearing habits of historical England. Henry VIII strode into his pages, exclaiming: 'God's death, my lords!' Toying with Nell Gwyn and half a dozen spaniels, Charles II was never tired of swearing: 'Odd's fish'. Lesser personages peppered the books with ' 'Sblood', ' 'Sdeath', ' 'Swounds', 'Zooks'. There was one who swore 'by the gallipots of Galen'. I got into trouble at school by repeating the words of the ancient nobility and royalty. The worst moment was on the cricket field when I was overheard calling somebody a 'lascivious varlet'.

QUESTIONS

1. What impression of the writer's personality does this passage convey?

2. Comment on the writer's use of diction and metaphors.

3. The writer of this passage became a professional man of letters. What details of the passage point to such a future development?

4. How would you describe the tone of this passage? Serious? Good humoured? Cynical? Give reasons for your answer.

5. How would you describe the writer's treatment of his subject matter?

6. Write a short piece describing your own introduction to the habit of reading.

◖ LOST CHILDREN by POLLY DEVLIN*

There's a wasps' nest outside my window, beautiful and strange. It looks ghostly but is wildly alive, an edifice built of layers of frail white stuff spun out of their bodies and glued by something so strong that it withstands the winds that blow from all quarters, My memories of my daughters are like that. Layer after layer of tough, living alien filaments spun into the fabric of my life. And like the nest, if I probe too closely the memories fly out and sting me: regrets, laughter, anger, joy, rage, guilt, happiness. Things I didn't do: worse — things I did.

Early on I devised a fairly simple method of memorising particular moments. I would look hard at three blonde heads soldered over a book, or a four-year-old Rose in yellow sou'wester and little else running through the rain, Bay in tutu that didn't fit, Daisy solemn in a lilac negligée, and register the mental snapshot. The next day it would have gone, overlaid by new realities.

Yet now that they have grown up I have only to close my eyes and those images are there, lost children, running away. I know those children. I know all about them. Where are they? And perhaps even more telling, where are the images of them when they were in their teens? That epoch went on for years and was crammed with scenes that would make Quentin Tarantino quail. Didn't I register those? Did I heck. I closed my eyes and looked away but they shoot up unbidden in nightmares.

---

* *The Irish Times*, Oct. 24, 1998

How did it happen? One minute you are a young woman in New York working for Diana Vreeland on *Vogue* with few responsibilities and a future that belongs only to you and the next minute your future has become irrevocably linked to three solipsistic blobs who have no idea that you exist outside of their needs and who are your hostages to fortune; you can't dump them — something that always appealed to me in affairs of the heart if they got boring. You can't reason with them and worst of all your love for them is unconditional. From a small apartment on Fifth Avenue next door to the Guggenheim, I found myself translated to deepest Shiredom with a husband and snap snap snap three children without any practice or training.

They had no practice, I had no training. I was lost in a new continent marked Here There Be Tygers. Rose was two years old when Daisy was born and Daisy was just over one when I found Bay was making an unscheduled appearance. It was all touch and go for a good many years and I remember once at the beginning driving into Bath one morning and remembering as I parked that I had a baby and she was sleeping in an empty house some 20 miles away.

There are faint but warning tremors quite early on, but they all point in the opposite direction; you run away from the epicentre only to find you are in the volcano; that first school, for example, where they must be exactly like the other girls — with the Barbie dolls and the white knee-length ankle socks and right backpack; and I remember Rose plaintively asking me (rather as Prince Charles asked Diana why she couldn't be more like Fergie) why I couldn't be more like Margaret's mum; when I sought out this paragon template to model myself on her I found that she sported an esoteric line in fancy bedroom slippers with red pompoms and could (and did) roll a cigarette from one end of her mouth to the other while singing Roy Orbison songs and frying hamburgers. But this desperate conformity is a bluff; they are planning another route entirely.

Nothing prepares you for the roller coaster ride as you simultaneously become the mother of adolescents, stop being best beloved and enter the dark night of the soul. You become an odious liability who gets it *soooo* wrong, mutter mutter, whereas before you were always miraculously right.

Do you remember those poor citizens of Pompeii going about their daily business, sucking their teeth and looking at shopping lists while a monster that would engulf grumbled quietly to itself and one day erupted and they were buried in disaster? Having an adolescent is something like that; although most of us walking wounded do crawl out from under the big dump eventually.

Looking back from a place of greater safety, it does seem as though one minute they are dependent, round adorables who think you are God, and the next they are fierce, black-rimmed creatures with smoke and steam rising from their bodies, crouching in the corners of your house and staring out at you like something from Gormenghast, and wishing you were, if not dead, then far, far away in a place where you couldn't shame them by your very existence — an embarrassment compounded by the sheer embarrassment of you knowing so much about them. And rather like Groucho Marx, who wanted to be able to buy back his introduction to someone he didn't like so he need never say he had met them, so they want to jettison all the Stuff that has clogged up behind you and them and start out clear, preferably as orphans or as refugees in Kerala.

There are certain epiphanies in the journey when you are at you wit's end and don't know what to do. Don't ever be afraid to ask for help. One such moment was when my eldest daughter was attending an expensive boarding school in Wiltshire. In face, all three were incarcerated in these atavistic establishments which if I had my way I would have absolutely nothing to do with; but, *mea culpa*, there they were. Termtime, as a consequence, was lullingly quiet and I regained a bit of myself. As I walked along Sloane Square to do something amazing such as buying a colander at Peter Jones, on a Wednesday morning in Michelmas term, when my daughter was in the bosom of Cranborne School, all 5 foot 10 inches of her, masses of flaming preRaphaelite hair gummed into spikes, eyes Gothicised, was legging it in fishnets across the said Square.

I watched her progress down the King's Road, open-mouthed; hers was clamped around a cigarette. Reader, what would you do? Let me give you a piece of advice. Always avoid confrontation. That Friday when I went to her school, ostensibly to pick her up for the weekend, I took her away for good. She never went back.

That weekend we, both her parents, were in our sittingroom when an apparition loomed above us in the doorway. A black wigwam topped by a white and totemic thingy. It steadied itself in the doorway and through a haze of livid rage I perceived by beloved daughter, her head shaved — the white was her skull, the green was a Mohican — dressed in a black, wool tent. This, as I later discovered, was a hideously expensive garment from a now defunct fashion house called Body Map. A less appropriate name could never be found.

Seeing her, I found myself in uncharted territory, a place where rage knew no bounds, where feral things lived. Hair is a sexy thing. Its importance goes deep into the feminine psyche. You've only to think how much we spend on removing it at one end and growing it at the other to know that it's not just decaying protein.

My rage was beyond rage. I wanted to sink my teeth in her neck, the one I had so often kissed as a baby.

She said, defiant as you like: "I can see you don't like it?" Like it? Like it? Her father knew a fight to the death was about to take place, and, drawing from the great well of mannerly Englishness within himself, said carefully: "Darling, it's very interesting." I was so tickled by this reaction — even in my rage it seemed a metaphor for our national characteristics — that my anger fizzled out, and I only just managed not to let laughter bubble out hysterically. (Ridicule is the easiest and most contemptible thing to use against teenagers and I used it all the time. No Queensberry rules in these battles.)

At my wit's end I turned to the best and asked St Paul's Girls' School to take pity on us both. I practically swung a bell and wore a hood outside their gates; I knew there wasn't the faintest hope but I fossicked on and when Rose turned up for an interview with Mrs Brigstocke and Miss Gough (God bless them) at St Paul's they turned not a hair, (And is there a happy ending, I hear you cry? Yes, yes. Straight A's and on to King's College, Cambridge and loadsa hair). I could quote many such incidents, so could every parent. It isn't funny when you're going through it; you wonder will you ever all get out intact the other side.

You become accustomed to being the subject of anxious scrutiny in case you do the wrong thing; and be warned that no matter what you do you can't do the right one. When I see young mothers oblivious to the reign of terror that lies ahead of them I want to warn them to get out the armour plating, close their minds, stop up their ears, because those little angels will become big demons, adept at searching out vulnerability, will find any chink and get in there fast and painfully. They have to; they are growing up and you are standing in their way.

You cannot envisage a time when your knowledge of their past will become valuable, their archeology. You are their enemy, but what's worse you are their rival, and one who has already had the man of their early dreams. Your sexuality troubles, annoys and revolts them; their desire for you to conform progresses far beyond wanting to be like Margaret's mother; they want you to be like her grandmother. And never forget they play dirty; you conform in every detail, i.e. you must shop exclusively in Marks and Spencer in the beige department of Soft Furnishings; you must never ever draw attention to yourself; you must apologise profusely even when people are doing you a Great Wrong; they, on the other hand, look like a mixture of Coco the Clown and Lola Montez and manners are a plot hatched by the middle-aged to repress creativity and spontaneity.

If you ever suspected they were a switch at birth, this is when you know it for certain. Quite suddenly their living quarters become like the caves at Lascaux. Ancient things on walls, darkness, heaps of noisome clothes, piles of rubbles. Precious rubbish, you understand. By analysing the magma in two of my daughters' rooms I could get clues about what they had been doing where, like an archeological dig. Not with Daisy's, though; she went about her adolescence in a different way. She just vanished.

In some ways I think the most difficult to come to terms with are those who don't fight, who don't rebel — (the rebels, at least, are still engaging with you) — but who silently slip away, withdraw from encounters and leave their body pods behind. Do you know that poem by Seamus Heaney about the hare?

> *Choose one set of tracks and track a hare*
> *Until the prints stop just like that, in snow.*
> *End of the line — Smooth drifts, where did she go?*
> *Back on her tracks of course, then took a spring*
> *Yards off to the side; clean break; no scent or sign.*

Daisy was like that; all the evidence of her was there. Room like an ice palace; impeccable girl; but the child I knew had gone, vanished. Eerie. She just evaded me; she was almost amiable in her psychic removal. When she came back she was an extraordinary person and grown up. Bay and Rose did their growing up in full view and often locked in mortal combat. That was the other thing I had no notion of. The violence that rampages between adolescents. They maul each other and half an hour later are united against the world. You being the world at that moment, although at other times you are an insane speck to irritate their world vision.

I'm glad it's over; the journey took a long time and on the way I lost my youth, sod it. The people I have back are amazing individuals. I am no longer the oracle or the nerd, the diviner or the know-nothing, neither the solution nor the problem. Now I'm a person they love; but where once I went ahead and they followed, now I follow in their footsteps, an old page-girl to their young St Wenceslas. I have all the time in the world and all the space I could need. I want them back.

1. Do you think that Polly Devlin in her article is fair in her presentation of teenagers and their attitude towards their parents? Give your own personal views.

2. What impression does the article give you of Polly Devlin as a mother? Explain how you form that impression.

3. How would you describe the style of this article? Chatty? Formal? etc.

4. Why do you think Polly Devlin concludes her article with the statement, 'I want them back'? What indications are given throughout the article that she will arrive at this conclusion?

5. Imagine that you are Daisy at the time she left home. Write a letter to a friend explaining why you are leaving home.

6. How representative do you think Polly Devlin was as a mother of teenagers?

7. How would you describe the tone of the article? Illustrate your answer with quotation or references.

8. What do we learn about the writer from the references and allusions in this article?

◀ FROM ANGELA'S ASHES by FRANK McCOURT*

Mam says, I'm a martyr for the fags and so is your father.

There may be a lack of tea or bread in the house but Mam and Dad always manage to get the fags, the Wild Woodbines. They have to have the Woodbines in the morning and any time they drink tea. They tell us every day that we should never smoke, it's bad for your lungs, it's bad for your chest, it stunts your growth, and they sit by the fire puffing away. Mam says, If 'tis a thing I ever see you with a fag in your gob I'll break your face. They tell us the cigarettes rot your

---

* *Angela's Ashes* by Frank McCourt (Flamingo, HarperCollins, 1997)

teeth and you can see they're not lying. The teeth turn brown and black in your heads and fall out one by one. Dad says he has holes in his teeth big enough for a sparrow to raise a family. He has a few left but he gets them pulled at the clinic and applies for a new set. When he comes home with the new set he shows his big new white smile that makes him look like an American and whenever he tells us a ghost story by the fire he pushes the lower teeth beyond his lip to his nose and frightens the life out of us. Mam's teeth are so bad she has to go to Barrington's Hospital to have them all pulled at the same time and when she comes home she is holding at her mouth a rag bright with blood. She has to sit up all night because you can't lie down when your gums are pumping blood or you'll choke in your sleep. She says she'll give up smoking entirely when this bleeding stops but she needs one puff of a fag this minute for the comfort that's in it. She tells Malachy go to Kathleen O'Connell's shop and ask her would she ever let her have five Woodbines till Dad collects the dole on Thursday. If anyone can get the fags out of Kathleen, Malachy can. Mam says he has the charm, and she tells me, There's no use sending you with your long face and your father's odd manner.

When the bleeding stops and Mam's gums heal she goes to the clinic for her false teeth. She says she'll give up the smoking when her new teeth are in but she never does. The new teeth rub on her gums and make them sore and the smoke of the Woodbines eases them. She and Dad sit by the fire when we have one and smoke their cigarettes and when they talk their teeth clack. They try to stop the clacking by moving their jaws back and forth but that only makes it worse and they curse the dentists and the people above in Dublin who made the teeth and while they curse their teeth clack. Dad claims that these teeth were made for the rich people in Dublin and didn't fit so they were passed on to the poor of Limerick who don't care because you don't have much to chew when you're poor anyway and you're grateful you have any class of a tooth in your head. If they talk too long their gums get sore and the teeth have to come out. Then they sit talking by the fire with their faces collapsed. Every night they leave the teeth in the kitchen in jam jars filled with water. Malachy wants to know why and Dad tells him it cleans them. Mam says, No, you can't have teeth in your head while you're sleeping for they'll slip and choke you to death entirely.

The teeth are the cause of Malachy going to Barrington's Hospital and me having an operation. Malachy whispers to me in the middle of the night, do you want to go downstairs and see if we can wear the teeth?

The teeth are so big we have trouble getting them into our mouths but Malachy won't give up. He forces Dad's upper teeth into his mouth and can't get them out again. His lips are drawn back and the teeth make a big grin. He looks like a monster in a film and it makes me laugh but he pulls at them and grunts, Uck, uck, and tears come to his eyes. The more he goes, Uck, uck, the harder I laugh till Dad calls from upstairs, What are you boys doing? Malachy runs from me, up the stairs, and now I hear Mam and Dad laughing till they see he can choke on the teeth. They both stick their fingers in to pull out the teeth but Malachy gets frightened and makes desperate uck, uck sounds. Mam says, We'll have to take him to the hospital, and Dad says, he'll take him. He makes me go in case the doctor has questions because I'm older than Malachy and that means I must have started all the trouble. Dad rushes through the streets with Malachy in his arms and I try to keep up. I feel sorry for Malachy up there on Dad's shoulder, looking back at me, tears on his cheeks and Dad's teeth bulging in his mouth. The doctor at Barrington's hospital says, No bother. He pours oil into Malachy's mouth and has the teeth out in a minute. Then he looks at me and says to Dad, Why is that child standing there with his mouth hanging open?

Dad says, That's a habit he has, standing with his mouth open.

The doctor says, Come here to me. He looks up my nose, in my ears, down my throat, and feels my neck.

The tonsils, he says. The adenoids. They have to come out. The sooner the better or he'll look like an idiot when he grows up with that gob wide as a boot.

Next day Malachy gets a big piece of toffee as a reward for sticking in teeth he can't get out and I have to go to the hospital to have an operation that will close my mouth.

QUESTIONS

1. One reviewer of *Angela's Ashes* has written: 'The most remarkable thing about Frank McCourt, apart from his survival, is his lack of sorrowfulness. *Angela's Ashes* sings with irreverent Limerick wit. It makes you smile at the triumph of the storyteller, a tougher specimen who escaped Limerick's teeming alleys through intelligence and cunning and lived to tell the tale.'

   Discuss this assessment, basing your answer on the above excerpt from the book.

2.   What kind of family life does Frank McCourt portray in the above excerpt? Support your views with references to specific details.

3.   How would you describe the style of the above writing? In your answer, make reference to sentence structure, vocabulary, idioms, similes, metaphors, etc.

4.   What impression of the personality of the narrator does the above excerpt convey?

5.   Are there any details in the excerpt that might suggest to you that the narrator is 'embroidering' or concealing the harsh realities of the life he is dealing with?

TOPICS FOR NARRATIVE/PERSONAL WRITING

Many topics may be treated in either an argumentative or personal form. The personal form may be narrative (a fictional story) or dramatic. The simple test for knowing whether or not it is appropriate and allowable to use these forms is to feel satisfied that your chosen topic can be considered the theme of the narrative or dramatic essay you have selected. If, for example, you choose 'Famine' as your topic, and you choose to write a personal narrative on this topic, 'famine' should be the theme of the narrative you compose.

1.   Summer holidays
2.   The lighter side of school life
3.   A character sketch of a most unusual person
4.   Feeling unwanted
5.   Dialling a wrong number
6.   Learning the hard way
7.   Leaving school
8.   Mischief-making
9.   Hitch-hiking
10.   The good neighbour
11.   My most valuable possession(s)
12.   Boredom
13.   The green door at the top of the stairs

14. 'I was there'

15. Late for a date

16. In court

17. When the music stopped

18. That Monday morning feeling

19. The end of a friendship

20. Living dangerously

21. Falling in love

22. The new man

23. Silence

24. Memories

25. Raindrops

26. One Christmas ...

27. The joy of being young

28. The take-away

29. The main pleasures of my life

30. Hairstyles

31. What might have been

32. Murder most foul

33. Ny first date

34. When I am old

35. A place in the sun

36. From rags to riches

37. A dream come true

38. My street

39. A holiday that went wrong

40. Reading the newspapers

41. If there were no television

42. Family joys and woes

43. A visit to the grandparents

44. Winning the lottery

45. The pleasures of country life

46. Sounds of our time

47. In the stillness of the night

48. Learning a foreign language

49. We never did *that* when we were young

50. In the eye of the storm

THE AESTHETIC
USE OF LANGUAGE:
(A) POETRY

The answer to this old bugbear of a question has to be that the word 'poetry' has meant different things at different times in different cultures. Hence the variety of answers which the question has produced.

In ancient civilisations such as those of Greece and Rome, or indeed Ireland or Iceland, long poems that tell the story of the exploits of a hero were known as *epic poems*. And centuries later in other countries these epic poems were imitated and were appreciated and are still appreciated as poetry.

In ancient Rome the writer Lucretius wrote a philosophical work, *De rerum natura* ('Concerning the nature of the Universe'), which was appreciated by his contemporaries as poetry. And also in ancient Rome the poet Virgil wrote what is in effect a text on agriculture in the form of poetry.

In ancient Ireland poets were considered genealogists whose function it was to keep a record in poetic form of notable families who in return patronised them.

In our own time, poetry, or at least verse-form (that is, metre, rhyme, etc.) is used in the *in memoriam* verses that appear in newspapers.

These different functions of poetry have resulted in different kinds of poems. But before analysing the different kinds of poems, it is important to understand first of all what these kinds of poems share to justify their description as 'poems'.

A WORKING DEFINITION

In its most fundamental sense, poetry is a memorable way of saying, singing or writing something that is worth remembering. In short, poetry is memorable speech, written or spoken.

This definition contains two essential elements:

1. The **memorability** of poetry.
2. The **value** of what is made memorable.

Now, these two elements, although they may sometimes be analysed separately, are in practice (that is, as the reader encounters them in the poem) usually experienced in combination, functioning together in harness. Indeed, it has often been argued that the more easily separable the two elements are, the poorer or weaker the poem is as a poem.

NURSERY RHYMES

Nursery rhymes or nonsense verses are usually extremely memorable. However, when it comes to the question of their value, there can be conflict of opinion. Some people are of the view that this kind of poetry is no more than a harmless device for amusing children. Other people have argued that this in itself is of worthwhile value. Others still have attempted to show that nonsense verses and nursery rhymes can be decoded so that they yield valuable insights into human experience or interesting comment on historical characters or events.

LITTLE JACK HORNER

To illustrate this, we can take the following example of one of the best known nursery rhymes:

> Little Jack Horner,
> Sat in a corner
> Eating his Christmas pie.
> He put in his thumb
> And pulled out a plum
> And said: 'What a good boy am I!'

Now here is what the famous poet, novelist and critic, Robert Graves, has to say about it:

Francis Horner, Scottish economist and member of Parliament during the Napoleonic Wars, was one of the few thoroughly honest statesmen of his day; he even refused a Treasury secretaryship in 1811 because he could not afford to live on the salary. In 1810 he had been secretary to the Parliamentary Committee which investigated inflation and persuaded the House to check the issue of paper-currency unsupported by bullion. Horner exercised a moral as well as an intellectual influence on his fellow-members, which galled the Whig Opposition. A 'plum' in the slang of the time was £100,000; it appeared even in such sober reports as 'The revenue is about £90 plum, to be increased by funding.' But here critical caution is needed. Though the Whigs may have mischievously applied the rhyme to Horner, as an accusation that he had secretly enriched himself by bribes from the City, while protesting his incorruptibility, it was already at least a century old. Henry Carey quotes it in his *Namby Pamby* satire on Ambrose Phillips in 1725. The Wiltshire Horners were a rich family who had profited from Henry VIII's dissolution of the monasteries, and seem to have been notorious for their self-righteousness.[1]

We can see that 'Little Jack Horner' is more than a nonsense rhyme. Whatever we decide to make of nursery rhymes and nonsense verse, the fact of the matter is that they have survived mainly because of their memorable form, their use of rhythm (metre, etc.) and rhyme.

METRE

The measurement of rhythm in poetry is called metre (the word comes the Greek 'metron', meaning 'a measure'). Until this present century almost all poetry in English was measured or metered, using groups of syllables called *metric feet*. For instance, all of Shakespeare's plays are written in *iambic feet*, that is to say, in feet of two syllables, the first of which is unstressed and the second stressed.

WORDS USED TO DISCUSS SOUND IN POETRY

Rhyme. The repetition of the same sounds, usually at the end of two or more lines.
For example: store/lore; home/ loam; much/ such

Alliteration. The repetition of the same consonant sounds.
For example: <u>F</u>ull <u>f</u>athom <u>f</u>ive thy <u>f</u>ather lies

---

[1] from *The Crowning Privilege* by Robert Graves (Penguin Books, 1969)

Assonance. The rhyming of vowel sounds.

For example: n<u>ow</u>, h<u>ou</u>r, s<u>ou</u>nd, sh<u>ow</u>er.

Onomatopeia. The use of sounds of words to suggest their sense.

For example: *The murmur of bees in the immemorial elms.*

THERE ARE BASICALLY THREE KINDS OF POEMS:

1. **Narrative Poems**: poems that tell stories
2. **Descriptive Poems**: poems that describe people or places
3. **Reflective Poems**: poems that express the poet's thoughts or feelings

Sometimes these three types are clearly distinctive, but often each type contains elements of the other two.

MORE KINDS OF POETRY

Pastoral Poetry. This is usually a mixture of narrative and descriptive poetry with a dramatic element added. It was once believed that poetry originated among shepherds and pastors.

Didactic Poetry. This is poetry that attempts to teach a moral lesson.

Satiric Poetry. This is a poetry of social criticism that uses mockery and ridicule.

The Ballad. The ballad is a narrative poem that tells a popular story. The old ballads were simple, direct and vigorous. The characters were presented simply and the rhythm of the poem was usually fast. Most ballads date from the eighteenth century. The word 'ballad' means a 'song' to which people could dance. No one is certain whether ballads were written by individuals or by the community, whereas folk-songs are made by the whole people and not by individuals.

The genuine **folk-song** has little or no conscious art. It is anonymous and a product of the community.

The Epic. This ballad tends to be objective. It highlights the qualities of the hero. It uses imagination and memory. It begins by stating what it is about to sing. It tells a story without making any moral comment. It usually contains lots of dialogue. It makes much use of action.

SOME FEATURES OF THE EPIC:

- The epic is a long narrative poem dealing with the exploits of some hero or heroes.
- Epic poetry tends to be objective; it describes without analysing.
- It attributes the hero with superhuman qualities.
- An epic usually begins by introducing what it is going to deal with.

Allegory. There is a literal level of meaning and a parallel symbolic level. The greatest allegory in any literature is probably Dante's *Divine Comedy*, in which the poet takes us on a journey of the soul through a world of sin, suffering and salvation. Each is represented by symbols, for example 'worldliness' is represented by a Dark Wood of Terror.

The Lyric. This is a short poem that is primarily concerned with the expression of the poet's feelings and thoughts as these are engaged in an experience. Whereas other kinds of poetry tend to be objective, the lyric is subjective.

KINDS OF LYRIC

- Religious lyric
- Patriotic lyric
- Love lyric
- Nature lyric
- Lament or Elegy
- The Sonnet

The Petrarchan Sonnet. The sonnet is a special kind of lyric. The Italian form of the sonnet is known as the Petrarchan Sonnet. It consists of two parts: an octave (eight lines) and a sextet (six lines); it has no final couplet.

The letters **A, B, C,** etc. are used to indicate rhyme; each letter stand for a different rhyme.

The rhyming scheme of the Petrarchan sonnet may be

(a) **ABBA ABBA CD CD CD**

(b) **ABBA ABBA CDE CDE**

The Shakespearian Sonnet. This consists of three quatrains (groups of four lines) and finishes with a rhyming couplet.

ABAB CDCD EFEF GG

FIGURES OF SPEECH USED IN DISCUSSING POETRY

Simile: a comparison of one thing with another; introduced by the words 'like' or 'as'.
For example: He roared like a lion.

Heroic or **Extended Simile**: a comparison elaborated to great length; this kind of simile is frequently found in epic poems.

Metaphor: a comparison that leaves out the word 'like' and 'as'.
For example: 'The Valley of Sackcloth'.

Personification: treating something inanimate as a living thing.
For example: 'O Wild West Wind, thou breath of autumn's being'.

Pathetic Fallacy: Treating something inanimate as though it had human feelings.
For example: The sky wept tears for the slain.

Paradox: An apparent contradiction used to get the reader's attention.
For example: The death of sin is the birth of grace.

Climax: The build-up of tension to a peak of intensity.

Anti-climax: A let-down or disappointment of an expectation.

Circumlocution: A roundabout way of expressing something; the use of more words than are necessary.

HOW TO READ A POEM

A poem may
- tell a **story**
- make a **statement**
- express an **idea**
- communicate a **feeling** or **feelings**
- reveal an insight into human **experience**

A poem may do one or all of these at the same time.

Roughly speaking, there are two stages in responding to a poem:

1. **Exposition and Analysis**: Understanding the poet's **intention** or **meaning**.

   Things to consider:
   - the **occasion** of the poem
   - the **historical context** of the poem (when, where and by whom the poem was written)
   - compiling a **glossary** or framework of the **references** or **allusions** in the poem (such as references to classical mythology, philosophical ideas, natural sciences such as botany, etc.); looking up **unfamiliar words**
   - identifying the **subject matter** of the poem
   - working out the **theme** of the poem

2. **Critical Assessment**: Making a **judgment** about how well or badly you think the poem has been realised or has fulfilled the poet's intention or meaning; the value you place on the experience of reading the poem.

   Things to consider:
   - the **relevance** and **importance** of the poem's **theme**
   - the poem's use of **similes, metaphors, symbols**
   - effects of **rhythm** and **rhyme**
   - a **comparison** of the poem with another poem by the same poet or a poem by some other poet
   - appreciation of any **originality** (of presentation, technique or content) in the poem

RESPONDING TO A POEM

FELIX RANDAL by GERARD MANLEY HOPKINS

Felix Randal the farrier, O he is dead then? my duty all ended,
Who have watched his mould of man, big-boned and hardy-handsome
Pining, pining, till time when reason rambled in it and some
Fatal four disorders, fleshed there, all contended?

Sickness broke him. Impatient he cursed at first, but mended

5

Being anointed and all; though a heavenlier heart began some

Months earlier, since I had our sweet reprieve and ransom

Tendered to him. Ah well, God rest him all road ever he offended!

This seeing the sick endears them to us, us too it endears.

My tongue had taught thee comfort, touched had quenched thy tears,   10

Thy tears that touched my heart, child, Felix, poor Felix Randal;

How far from then forethought of, all thy more boisterous years,

When thou at the random grim forge, powerful amidst peers,

Didst fettle for the great grey drayhorse his bright and battering sandal!

EXPOSITION AND ANALYSISI

HISTORICAL CONTEXT

Gerard Manley Hopkins was born in Stratford, Essex, on July 28, 1844. He was the eldest of eight children of a prosperous, middle-class family. In some respects the Hopkins household was not typical. The poet's father, Manley Hopkins, besides his professional interests, wrote books and was fascinated with arcane or unusual knowledge. The arts had a strong presence in the family, and these included music and drawing as well as literature. Two of Hopkins' brothers went on to become professional painters. Hopkins' mother was a devout and thoughtful woman.

While Hopkins was at Highgate School in London, he distinguished himself as a brilliant and diligent student, and he was also recognized as a person of extreme independence and strength of character. Once, to prove his argument that people drink too much, he refused any liquids for a full week. But Hopkins was not only interested in his academic studies: he also sketched and wrote poetry for which he won the school Poetry Prize in 1860. Despite all this, Hopkins confessed that he did not enjoy his time in school.

After Highgate, Hopkins went up to Balliol College, Oxford, in 1863. He had chosen to study Classics (Latin and Greek), and in this subject he achieved such distinction as an undergraduate that, had he chosen to, he could have become, as his Professor of Greek, Benjamin Jowett, believed, a famous classical scholar. In Oxford, Hopkins met the doctor-poet, Robert Bridges, with whom he maintained a lifelong friendship.

During Hopkins' period in Oxford in the 1860s, a religious debate, called the Oxford Movement, was taking place there. Essentially, the debate concerned a growing division within the Anglican or Established Church between Broad Church liberals who wanted the Church of England to become more 'progressive' by ridding itself of some of its traditional forms of worship, and High Church Anglicans who were intent on defending these traditions. Hopkins sided with the traditionalists and this decision led him in due course towards Roman Catholicism, which seemed to Hopkins to offer a stronger defence of traditional Anglican values than the Anglican Church itself. The example of John Henry Newman (who eventually became a Cardinal), an Anglican who converted to Catholicism, and a powerful intellectual force in the Oxford of Hopkins' time, exercised a strong influence on Hopkins in his painful decision (his family opposed it) not only to join the Catholic Church, but also to become a Jesuit.

Always a man of sincere and uncompromising principles as well as great intelligence and artistic talent, Hopkins felt that in deciding to devote his life to the service of God, he must totally reject the things of the world, and this included his passion for art which he now saw as a glorification of the world. Consequently, in 1868, when he entered the Novitiate of the Society of Jesus, he destroyed all he had written that was still in his possession, and, as he wrote in his Journal, 'resolved to write no more, as not belonging to my profession, unless by the wish of my superiors.'

Hopkins' rejection of his artistic self, however, was not to last. His interest in poetry continued and while he was in Wales studying theology he found time to learn some Welsh and acquaint himself with classical Welsh poetry. It was while he was in Wales, in December 1875, that he was asked by the Rector of St Beuno's College, the seminary in which he was studying, to write a poem on the occasion of the sinking of the 'Deutschland', a ship that was wrecked in the mouth of the Thames and which had on board five Franciscan nuns who were being exiled by the anti-Catholic laws in Germany. In writing his poem 'The Wreck of the Deutschland', Hopkins broke a seven-year poetic silence.

But the groundwork of this astonishing poetic production had already been laid by Hopkins. During his theological studies, Hopkins had discovered, to his great delight, the writings of Duns Scotus (*c.* 1265–1304 AD). Scotus placed enormous emphasis on the individuality of all created things, seeing in such infinite individuality the reflected glory of the Creator. In this way, Hopkins came to find a theological justification for his interest in the actual reality of created things. To write poems in celebration of things could therefore be viewed by him as an act, not of artistic self-indulgence, but of praising God the Creator, and, thus, a form of prayerful homage.

Hopkins' first duties were carried out in Dublin where he was appointed Professor of Classics of the Royal University (later, University College, Dublin). He was not happy in Dublin however. Throughout his life, Hopkins suffered weak or poor health and nervous exhaustion brought on by over-work. In Dublin he found himself, an Englishman, isolated from many of his Jesuit confrères by the growing Irish nationalism of the time; this isolation was aggravated by the absence of his family and his English friends. Hopkins died of enteric fever in Dublin in 1889 and he is buried in the Jesuit communal plot in Glasnevin Cemetery in Dublin.

OCCASION OF POEM

Hopkins has heard the news that a blacksmith parishioner of his, Felix Randal, whom he has been attending during the man's terminal sickness (perhaps cancer), has died. He recalls Randal's wasting away, his once fine physique becoming the shadow of itself, and recalls Randal's suffering.

He also recalls his own priestly relationship with the farrier. At first Randal bitterly resented the misfortune of his sickness and cursed his fate. But Hopkins' priestly ministrations brought him round to accepting his condition in a mood of Christian stoicism. Randal was a strong, able man and clearly the poet liked him.

GLOSSARY AND REFERENCES

1 *the farrier*: a shoeing blacksmith
my duty: Hopkins' duty as a ministering priest (e.g. hearing his confessions and giving him spiritual comfort)

2 *his mould of man*: his body; his manly shape
hardy handsome: tough, robust, strong and impressive in a manly way

3 *when reason rambled in it*: when Randal became delirious; when he was losing control of his mind

4 *fatal four disorders*: the illness which afflicted him
fleshed there: embedded in his flesh
all contended: the blacksmith's body in a rage of sickness, everything going wrong

5 *sickness broke him*: his spirit and will-power were broken by sickness

mended: became spiritually resigned to his fate; faced the facts of his illness

6 *heavenlier heart*: he became better disposed towards religion

7 *sweet reprieve*: the grace of extreme unction (last rites)

ransom: Christ's redemption of man (in the form of holy communion)

8 *all road ever he offended*: in his journey all through life, Randal had never offended or insulted anyone

9 In seeing the sick, we are reminded of the frailty of human nature and our compassion for our fellow human beings is thereby aroused; and from the sick person's point of view, the charity and compassion he is shown makes him kindly disposed towards other people.

10 Hopkins gave Randal both spiritual and emotional comfort.

11 Randal's response to Hopkins' solicitations and ministrations.

12 *how far from then forethought*: how far from Randal's mind (any prior knowledge of the illness which would afflict him)

all thy more boisterous years: during Randal's years of vigour and vitality

13 *random*: the forge was built of irregularly-shaped stones

powerful amidst peers: powerful even among the more powerful horses; strong even in comparison with the superior strength of the horse

14 *fettle*: prepare or make ready

drayhorse: a horse used for drawing carts

bright and battering sandal: the new horseshoe, shining and soon to be used battering the stones of the road

CRITICAL ASSESSMENT

THEME

Having presented the occasion of the poem, Hopkins goes on to meditate upon sickness. Rather than seeing it as a dreadful and hopeless misfortune, Hopkins finds something positive to say. The carer can respond to the sick person with compassion, the patient with gratitude for human kindness. Thus for all its horror, sickness, which is inevitable and part and parcel of the human condition, can be viewed as a humanising process and so made bearable.

Finally, Hopkins does not resort, as he might have done, to moralising. Instead, Hopkins the priest steps back and Hopkins the man registers his response in a touching lament for the transience of human life, the passing away of its splendid beauty. It is remarkable, but consistent with Hopkins' profoundly religious view of life, that a poem on sickness should conclude with such a magnificent image as that of 'the great grey drayhorse'.

ORIGINALITY

'Inscape' and 'Instress'

These two related terms are complex. Roughly speaking, by 'inscape' Hopkins means the pattern or form by which the inner nature or individuality (the *haecceitas* or 'thisness') of an object shows itself to our senses; that is to say, the pattern or qualities that reveals the individual or unique essence of an object.

'Instress' is the energetic impact of 'inscape' on the human sensibility, although it should not be understood entirely in terms of the senses, as the 'inscape' of an object is ultimately something beyond the senses. Hopkins sometimes uses the metaphor of fire to express his idea of 'instress': the moment in which occurs the impact of the 'inscape' on a sympathetic and perceptive observer. The religious or spiritual factor in all of this, so essential to Hopkins, cannot be accounted for in purely psychological or aesthetic terms.

The 'oddness' of Hopkins' poetic style should be understood with the above notions of 'inscape' and 'instress' firmly in mind. As Hopkins in his poems is attempting to register in language what is unique in what he is describing, he is at the same time compelled to mould language, in rhythm and diction, simile and metaphor, into a corresponding and expressive uniqueness. The poem as literary artifact must be for Hopkins as unique and individual as the object or experience it is its purpose to express.

❨ QUESTIONS AND SAMPLE ANSWERS

Question 1

How would you describe Hopkins' attitude towards Felix Randal? Support your answer with quotation from and reference to the poem.

Answer

Hopkins' attitude towards Randal is caring and affectionate. This is expressed in the grief of 'O he is dead then' and in the admiration implicit in Hopkins' description of Randal's splendid physique: 'his mould of man, big-boned and hardy-handsome'. More directly, Hopkins expresses his affection for Randal in his blessing and his declaration of the essential innocence and goodness of the farrier: 'God rest him all road ever he offended'. But perhaps the finest tribute Hopkins pays to Randal, which expresses his care and appreciation of the man, is to be found in the last lines of the poem in which Hopkins represents the farrier in all the splendour of his earlier physical presence when he stood 'powerful amidst peers', shoeing for the 'great grey drayhorse his bright and battering sandal'.

Question 2

What images in the poem convey the humanity of Hopkins' treatment of the farrier? Be specific in your references.

Answer

Hopkins' duty as a priest was to attend Randal in a ministering capacity, providing the dying man with spiritual comfort and solace. Hopkins did this with apparent success. As a priest, Hopkins might well be expected to go on to moralise about the importance of religion, exploiting the experience of attending Randal as so much raw material for the preaching of a religious lesson. Instead, Hopkins goes beyond his priestly, ministering role — while not lessening its importance in any way — to express a very human compassion for what has happened to Randal: the farrier's decline from a state of physical strength and splendour ('big-boned and hardy-handsome') to the physical disintegration brought on by his sickness. Hopkins' humanity is above all shown in this compassion for the human condition embodied and experienced in Randal.

Question 3

Relate the image of 'the great grey drayhorse' in the poem's last line to the figure of the farrier. What do you think Hopkins is trying to achieve in this connection?

Answer

Hopkins' poem finishes with the splendid image of the 'great grey drayhorse' which Randal has once shod with 'his bright and battering sandal'. As the poem is about sickness and death, among other things, it would be easy enough for Hopkins to conclude his poem with a dour moral warning or on a depressing note of sentimental pity. Hopkins, however, uses the image of the great drayhorse — a physically magnificent creature — to remind the reader, by association, of Randal's own past magnificent presence. Hopkins — running counter to the reader's expectations — insists on ending the poem positively in the celebration of the physical. And, extraordinarily, he does this without indulging in a false escapism. God's physical creation may perish, but at its finest — like Randal in his youthful past and the great grey drayhorse — being what God intended, it can be a thing of great beauty.

Question 4

Hopkins' attitude towards sickness is deeply Christian and human. How convincing do you find this? Give reasons for your answer.

Answer

Hopkins' attitude towards sickness is stated explicitly in line 9 when he says 'This seeing the sick endears them to us, us too it endears'. It is not difficult to recall contrary views of sickness: sickness as nothing but trouble for everyone, the cause of misery and alienation, producing resentment, bitterness and even hatred in both the sufferer and those whose duty, moral and emotional, it is to care. As a Christian, Hopkins sees sickness as an opportunity to show human love and compassion (based on Christ's commandment that we should love our neighbour as ourselves). Thus Hopkins' compassion may be viewed as spiritual and Christian in its motivation. However, Hopkins' emotional willingness to view Randal in his mortality, without exploiting it for the purpose of preaching a moral lesson, reveals his deep humanity. Perhaps, though, in the end, Hopkins' Christian values cannot be separated from his humanity because his humanity is so thoroughly permeated with his profoundly Christian values.

Question 5

Sickness, especially terminal sickness, is usually a depressing, even despairing experience for both the patient and family and friends. How does the poem show us that it may be otherwise?

Answer

It is common experience that sickness at its worst, in terminal illness, frequently reduces the victim and his or her carers to states of bitter resentment, anguished frustration and even suicidal despair. Hopkins argues — poetically — for a more positive or at least stoical view of sickness.

He describes Randal's initial reaction to his illness: 'Impatient he cursed at first'. Hopkins understands and accepts that reaction. It is all too human. But Hopkins also knows that sickness and death are part and parcel of the human condition. That being so, it is a question of coming to terms with the human condition itself, not just with some of its consequences. Hopkins sees human life in a Christian framework. Within that framework there is an acceptance of suffering and death, in the faith of spiritual salvation. It is Hopkins' faith in the 'sweet reprieve' of Christ's Redemption that sustains Hopkins and finally comforts Randal.

It is Hopkins' view, also, that the positive virtues of religious faith and compassion can be discovered through suffering. This, Hopkins argues, can be an alternative to hopelessness and despair.

QUESTIONS

1. Although Hopkins seems to have had in mind a specific individual when writing this poem, he has also managed to deal with a universal experience. How do you think he has achieved this? Support your answer with precise references to the poem.

2. Line 9 of the poem makes a challenging statement. How effectively do you think the poem supports that statement?

3. 'Hopkins addresses Felix Randal as a "child", yet he does so without offensive condescension, and it is possible for him to do this only because the experience of the poem is placed in a religious framework.' Explain what you understand by this statement, and then discuss it.

4. Trace the development of the poem from the opening line in which Hopkins tells of hearing the news of Randal's death.

5. How would you argue for the value of this poem to a reader who does not share Hopkins' religious convictions? Support your arguments with specific references to the poem.

POEMS FOR STUDY

(1) A REFUSAL TO MOURN THE DEATH, BY FIRE, OF A CHILD IN LONDON* by DYLAN THOMAS

Never until the mankind making
Bird beast and flower
Fathering and all humbling darkness
Tells with silence the last light breaking
And the still hour
Is come of the sea tumbling in harness

And I must enter again the round
Zion of the water bead
And the synagogue of the ear of corn
Shall I let pray the shadow of a sound
Or sow my salt seed
In the least valley of sackcloth to mourn
The majesty and burning of the child's death.
I shall not murder
The mankind of her going with a grave truth

Nor blaspheme down the stations of the breath
With any further
Elegy of innocence and youth.

Deep with the first dead lies London's daughter,
Robed in the long friends,
The grains beyond age, the dark veins of her mother,
Secret by the unmourning Thames.
After the first death, there is no other.

EXPOSITORY INTRODUCTION

Death, like love, has always been an obsessional subject for artists, as indeed it has been for all of humankind. It is the great challenging question that confronts human existence. And we all must come to terms with it sooner or later, one way or another. Dylan Thomas's poem may be seen as one such attempt to come to terms with the problem of death.

* from *Dylan Thomas: The Poems*, edited by Daniel Jones (J.M. Dent, London)

Thomas confronts death in the specific form of the burning to death of a young girl in London during the Second World War. But this specific form is incidental. It is death itself that engages Thomas's imagination. The confrontation is not between the young girl and death, but in fact between Thomas himself and death. As Thomas's critic, Elder Olson, has observed in his *The Poetry of Dylan Thomas*: 'Thomas's imagination could transport him anywhere, through all space and all time; but it is also true that, wherever it takes him, he sees nothing but himself.' Commenting on this poem by Thomas, Elder Olson writes: 'Moved by grief for a burned child, nobly and powerfully moved as he is, he does not suffer imaginatively the experience of the child, does not share in it in the least; he sees the pain and the horror from without, and the resolution he reaches is a resolution for him, not for the child.' Thomas is the same kind of subjective poet as Keats whom he admired from his earliest years: the world of his poetry is not the real world, but the projected world of his own imagination.

Death as a physical phenomenon is insurmountable. What may be overcome, however, is the moribund depression which contemplating death often produces. Coming to terms with death means triumphing over the morbidity that can engulf and destroy life through fear and anxiety. In 'A Refusal to Mourn' Thomas's resolution of the problem of death is through the ancient escapist notion of rebirth: one of the most deep-seated yearnings of the human personality. If one may be reborn again, then death scarcely matters. At worst, it is a mere hiatus or blank in existence.

Various writings on mythology, and particularly its psychological interpretation by such scholars as Jung and Rank, have revealed the antiquity of symbols of rebirth, and how these often involve images or symbols of water and earth and the idea of being surrounded by, enclosed in a small space. Frequently there is a sinking into the water of the sea or a descent into the earth: in other words, a return to the primary sources of life. Death is seen as a return to the mother's body, to be reborn again. This link between birth and death is evident in Job's 'Naked came I from my mother's womb and naked shall I return thither.'

Thomas's first long sentence, from line 1 to line 13, presents the reader with the perspective of time in which death must be viewed. This is not chronological time, the time of clocks and calendars, but the biblical or mythological time of Creation:

'In the beginning God created the heaven and the earth. And the earth was without form and void; and darkness was upon the face of the deep. And the Spirit of God moved upon the face of the waters. And God said, Let there be light; and there was light. And God saw the light, and it was good: and God divided the light from the darkness.'

It is out of darkness that all life came: mankind, bird, beast, flower (for this reason Thomas describes the darkness as 'mankind making' and 'bird, beast and flower/Fathering'). Out of light and the sea life also came. And when Thomas himself dies, his death will be a return to the flux of mothering nature ('the water bead' and 'the ear of corn', both cradling images). In this long sentence, Thomas is saying that he will not mourn the girl's death until life itself is at an end. At the same time he is setting up a mythopoeic context or fantasy into which we should accept his understanding of death.

Line 13 contains Thomas's almost outrageous defiance of death when he applies the word 'majesty' — in the same breath as 'burning' — to the child's death. The justification for this will come later in the poem.

In Thomas's godlike presentation of time, to mourn with talk of 'grave truth', the humanness, the naturalness of the child's going, would be to murder or reduce that humanness. To sigh ('the stations of the breath') over it would be to blaspheme its holiness, the sacredness of the process through which the child returns to her natural elements.

In the last stanza of the poem, Thomas returns more specifically to the child's death. The flames in which she was consumed are here described as 'long friends'. The Greek philosopher Heraclitus believed that fire was the basic element of the universe: fire is thus beyond age ('grains beyond age'), and it is the mother of all life ('dark veins of the mother') in that it is its basic element, out of which it comes into being and into which it returns. It is the 'holy fire' of Yeats's 'Sailing to Byzantium' and the 'nature's bonfire' of Hopkins' 'That Nature is a Heraclitean Fire'.

The poem's last line constitutes the final triumph of Thomas's imagination over death. It is birth, our emergence from our pre-natal state of elemental being, that is our real death. It is our first death, since our reabsorption into the mothering elements can scarcely be described as death, at least as it is usually understood.

Thomas's resolution of the problem of death, as worked out by him in 'A Refusal to Mourn', can be compared with many poems in many languages. In

English one easily thinks of Wordsworth's 'Loud is the Vale' and Keats's 'Ode to a Nightingale'. The last two stanzas of 'Loud is the Vale', in the vision of the Great Afterwards, provides a striking insight into Thomas's vision of that same place:

A Power is passing from the earth
To breathless Nature's dark abyss;
But when the great and good depart
What is it more than this —

That Man, who is from God sent forth,
Doth yet again to God return? —
Such ebb and flow must ever be,
Then wherefore should we mourn?

● QUESTIONS

1. What argument or arguments does Dylan Thomas give for his refusal to mourn the death of the child? How valid do you think these arguments are?

2. How would you describe the poet's attitude towards death?

3. Identify and discuss the religious language and ideas in the poem.

4. In the context of your overall reading of the poem, give your own interpretation of the poem's last line.

5. 'This poem has less to do with the death of the child than it has to do with Dylan Thomas himself.' Discuss this statement.

6. Compare and contrast Thomas's poem with any other poem you have read on the subject of death.

◀ (2) POEM by WILLIAM CARLOS WILLIAMS

By the road to the contagious hospital,
under the surge of the blue
mottled clouds driven from the
northeast — a cold wind. Beyond, the
waste of broad, muddy fields,
brown with dried weeds, standing and fallen,
patches of standing water,
the scattering of tall trees.

All along the road the reddish,
purplish, forked, upstanding, twiggy
stuff of bushes and small trees
with dead, brown leaves under them
leafless vines —

Lifeless in appearance, sluggish,
dazed spring approaches —

They enter the new world naked,
cold, uncertain of all
save that they enter. All about them
the cold, familiar wind —
Now the grass, tomorrow
the stiff curl of wild-carrot leaf.

One by one the objects are defined —
It quickens: clarity, outline of leaf,

But now the stark dignity of
entrance — Still, the profound change
has come upon them; rooted, they
grip down and begin to awaken.

1. How would you describe the theme of this poem?

2. Do you think that there is anything more than an accidental connection
    between the contagious hospital and what is later described in the poem?
    Argue your point of view.

3. How would you argue the case that this poem is a poem and not simply a
    piece of chopped up prose?

4. Although this poem is taken up largely with description, do you think that
    the poet is using description to make some sort of statement about life?
    What do you think that statement might be?

◀ (3) SERVANT BOY by SEAMUS HEANEY*

He is wintering out
the back-end of a bad year,
swinging a hurricane-lamp
through some outhouse;

a jobber among shadows.
Old work-whore, slave-
blood, who stepped fair-hills
under each bidder's eye

and kept your patience
and your counsel, how
you draw me into
your trail. Your trail

broken from haggard to stable,
a straggle of fodder
stiffened on snow,
comes first-footing
the back doors of the little
barons: resentful
and impenitent,
carrying the warm eggs.

---

* from *Selected Poems 1965-1975* by Seamus Heaney (Faber & Faber, London)

◖ (4) MESSENGER BOY IN THE HARDWARE STORE by M.J. SMITH*

for Peadar

The hand scarcely reaches to the counter.
While he waits, holding the indecipherable
slip, the mandated message,
he stares dumbly at the array of tools
beyond his ken, not ever for his use,
not fit for hands like his.
The tweed jacket's stained and torn;
its leathered elbows hint of school
where likely he was no success,
or else the jacket was not always his.

The way his body rests, limply,
against the counter
suggests defeat.
Spent matches,
a piece of string and a scrap of paper
litter the floor at his feet.

● QUESTIONS

1. Compare and contrast the above two poems in terms of theme, setting, mood, etc.

2. Describe Seamus Heaney's attitude towards the servant boy.

3. Work out the relationship between the last three lines of M.J. Smith's poem and the rest of the poem.

4. What do you think the two boys in the poems have in common?

5. Discuss the urban/rural differences evident in the two poems.

---

* from *Lost Genealogies & Other Poems* by Michael Smith (New Writers' Press, Dublin 1993)

◀ (5) AFTER APPLE-PICKING by ROBERT FROST*

My long two-pointed ladder's sticking through a tree

Toward heaven still,

And there's a barrel that I didn't fill

Beside it, and there may be two or three

Apples I didn't pick upon some bough.

But I am done with apple-picking now.

Essence of winter sleep is on the night,

The scent of apples: I am drowsing off.

I cannot rub the strangeness from my sight

I got from looking through a pane of glass

I skimmed this morning from the drinking trough

And held against the world of hoary grass.

It melted, and I let it fall and break.

But I was well

Upon my way to sleep before it fell,

And I could tell

What form my dreaming was about to take.

Magnified apples appear and disappear,

Stem end and blossom end,

And every fleck of russet showing clear.

My instep arch not only keeps the ache,

It keeps the pressure of a ladder-round.

I feel the ladder sway as the boughs bend.

And I keep hearing from the cellar bin

The rumbling sound

Of load on load of apples coming in.

For I have had too much

Of apple-picking: I am overtired

Of the great harvest I myself desired.

There were ten thousand thousand fruit to touch,

Cherish in hand, lift down, and not let fall.

For all

That struck the earth,

---

* from *Complete Poems of Robert Frost* (Holt, Rinehart & Winston Inc., New York)

No matter if not bruised or spiked with stubble,

Went surely to the cider-apple heap

As of no worth.

One can see what will trouble

This sleep of mine, whatever sleep it is.

Were he not gone,

The woodchuck could say whether it's like his

Long sleep, as I describe its coming on,

Or just some human sleep.

QUESTIONS

1. What is the significance of the farmer's dream after the labour of apple-picking?

2. What details in the poem nudge the reader toward interpreting the poem as more than a description of the farmer's day?

3. What suggests to you that the farmer's tiredness is more than a reference to his physical exhaustion after apple-picking?

4. Identify the references to the seasons in the poem and comment on their importance.

5. What impression do you form of the farmer? Would you say that he is a kind of country philosopher? How does his character and occupation lend weight to what he thinks?

THE AESTHETIC
USE OF LANGUAGE:
(B) FICTION

- Character
- Plot/ Story-line/ Narrative
- Atmosphere/ Setting/ Location
- Subject Matter
- Theme/ Meaning
- Dialogue
- Description

CHARACTER AND PLOT

There are two broad categories of fiction that are not always separable but are identifiable by the emphasis they place on either character or plot:

1. Fiction that is primarily concerned with character, with exploring the human personality, with answering questions about human motivation and behaviour. The fiction of writers such as Henry James and the great Russian novelist Fyodor Dostoyevski meets this description. Although both of these great novelists make use of plots in their fiction, what their characters do is generally subservient to the exploration of character.

2. Fiction that is primarily concerned with action, with what people do. Detective stories, thrillers and most popular fiction fall into this category. Characters are, of course, an essential ingredient of this kind of fiction, yet it is the actions they are involved in that principally engage the readers' attention and interest. The ins-and-outs of the plot or action stimulate our curiosity and intrigue us. The characters, such as detective-heroes, tend to be fixed from the beginning of the story and do not develop much as the story unfolds. They are like the pieces in the game of chess.

○ **CHARACTER**

The reader's impression of a character is created through:

- Descriptive details of the character's physical appearance: age, facial features, dress, etc.
- Traits of personality: Is the character trusting or calculating? Aggressive or passive? Bad-tempered or easy-going? etc.
- Social and cultural background: upper, middle, working class; profession or occupation; nationality; education; religious or moral values.

This information is communicated to the reader

- Directly by the author or narrator
- Directly by the character
- Indirectly by what the character does (action) and says (dialogue)
- Indirectly by other characters

◀ **ARTHUR MOREL**

Analyse your impression of Arthur Morel as he is portrayed in the following passage. Support your answer by reference to specific details of the presentation.

Arthur Morel was growing up. He was a quick, careless, impulsive boy, a good deal like his father. He hated study, made a great moan if he had to work, and escaped as soon as possible to his sport again.

In appearance he remained the flower of the family, being well made, graceful, and full of life. His dark brown hair and fresh colouring, and his exquisite dark blue eyes shaded with long lashes, together with his generous manner and fiery temper, made him a favourite. But as he grew older his temper became uncertain. He flew into rages over nothing, seemed unbearably raw and irritable.

His mother, whom he loved, wearied of him sometimes. He thought only of himself. When he wanted amusement, all that stood in his way he hated, even if it were she. When he was in trouble he moaned to her ceaselessly.

'Goodness, boy!' she said, when he groaned about a master who, he said, hated him, 'if you don't like it, alter it, and if you can't alter it, put up with it.'

from *Sons and Lovers* by D.H. Lawrence

● YOUR TURN

(Write at least 30 lines)

1.   Describe the physical appearance of a well-known public figure.

2.   You have been mugged by two thugs on your way home from school. Give a description of these characters as you would to the police.

3.   You have met for the first time your older brother's girlfriend. Write a description of her in a letter to a friend.

4.   Your parents have had a row about the company your sister is keeping. Describe this row so that you give an impression of your parents and also the impression of your sister that emerges from what your parents say about her in the course of the row.

5.   You have been on a blind date. Give your impression of the person you have been on the date with.

6.   A stranger in your area has aroused your suspicion. Give your impression of this person drawing attention to what in the person's behaviour has aroused your suspicion.

STEREOTYPING

Read again the description of sterotyping on page 42.

What details in the following portrait suggest to you that the character presented is a stereotype? Identify the stereotype.

His thinness was not of the natural kind, but artificial. His frame seemed big enough to support a man of half his weight again. It was the thinness of meanness. The lean face and shifty eyes, the thin pursed lips, the bony fingers, the slow cautious speech. His wealth was not a boon but an affliction to him, a disease that ravaged his life.

YOUR TURN

Present a stereotype picture of the following:

1. A school bully
2. An authoritarian teacher
3. A tough self-made wealthy person
4. An absentminded professor
5. A politician
6. A police officer
7. A pop-star
8. A vain TV celebrity
9. A drug addict
10. A soccer hooligan

PLOT / STORY-LINE / NARRATIVE

Plot is the course of the action charted by the story. For example, a character who witnesses a murder is observed by the murderer; the witness flees from the scene and the murderer is intent on tracking down and eliminating the witness. The plot of such a story will chart the efforts of the murderer to discover the identity and whereabouts of the witness and at the same time it will chart the efforts of the witness to escape the pursuit of the murderer.

A plot usually takes its starting-point from someone doing something or being in a problematic situation. That situation has to be resolved. But first there are obstacles to be overcome. The basic pattern is:

Situation

Complication(s)

Resolution

EXAMPLE:

Situation

A young tramp calls at a large neglected country house to ask for food in return for doing some odd jobs. An old woman answers the door. She likes the appearance of the tramp and gives him work to do. By the end of the day the tramp and the old woman are getting on well. The old woman invites the tramp to stay on to do more work. Within a couple of days they are firm friends. The situation looks good.

Complications

The old woman starts to irritate the tramp by mothering him. The tramp is becoming restless and wants to move on. One day the tramp sees the old woman take some banknotes out of a suitcase which seems to be full of money. The tramp decides to rob the money and disappear. He waits until the old woman goes to town. While he is robbing the money the old woman returns unexpectedly. She tries to reason with the tramp but he panics and pushes her aside. She falls and hits her head against a chair. The tramp discovers that she is dead. He takes the suitcase full of money and flees.

Resolution

The old woman had gone to town to change her will, leaving all her possessions to the young tramp whom she has seen as a replacement of her long-dead only son. She has given her lawyer a full description of the tramp. As soon as her death is discovered, a search is organised, the tramp is found and is arrested by the police.

● YOUR TURN

Present a stereotype picture of the following:

1. Outline the plot of a bank robbery.

2. Outline the plot of a love story.

3. Outline the plot of a rag-to-riches story.

4. Outline the plot of a survival-situation story.

5. Outline the plot of a murder/jealousy story.

6. Outline the plot of a ghost story.

7. Outline the plot of a story with a surprise ending.

8. Outline the plot of a science fiction story.

9. Outline the plot of a story dealing with family conflict.

10. Outline the plot of a story dealing with moral conflict.

ATMOSPHERE/ SETTING/ LOCATION

Atmosphere is created by description of the setting of the action. For example, two children on their way home from school decide to investigate the inside of a derelict house; the fearful bravado and innocence of the children are set against the unknown menace of the derelict house; the atmosphere is tense and threatening.

Analyse the **atmosphere** in the following passage. Refer to the writer's use of specific details to create that atmosphere.

> Dinner-time was now near, so Mr Dillet spent but five minutes in putting the lady and children into the drawing-room, the gentlemen into the dining-room, the servants into the kitchen and stables, and the old man back into his bed. He retired into his dressing-room next door, and we see and hear no more of him until something like eleven at night.
>
> His whim was to sleep surrounded by some of the gems of his collection. The big room in which we have seen him contained his bed: bath, wardrobe, and all the appliances of dressing were in a commodious room adjoining: but his four-poster, which itself was a valued treasure, stood in the large room where he sometimes wrote, and often sat, and even received visitors. Tonight he repaired to it in a highly complacent frame of mind.
>
> There was no striking clock within earshot — none on the staircase, none in the stable, none in the distant church tower. Yet it is indubitable that Mr Dillet was startled out of a very pleasant slumber by a bell tolling one.
>
> He was so much startled that he did not merely lie breathless with wide-open eyes, but actually sat up in bed.
>
> He never asked himself, till the morning hours, how it was that, though there was no light at all in the room, the Dolls' House on the kneehole table stood out with complete clearness.

> from *The Haunted Dolls' House* by M.R. James

Analyse your impression of the **setting** given in the following paragraphs. Discuss the writer's use of detail.

On the pleasant shore of the French Riviera, about halfway between Marseilles and the Italian border, stands a large, proud, rose-coloured hotel. Deferential palms cool its flushed facade, and before it stretches a short dazzling beach. Lately it has become a summer resort of notable and fashionable people; a decade ago it was almost deserted after its English clientele went north in April. Now, many bungalows cluster near it, but when this story begins only the cupolas of a dozen old villas rotted like water-lilies among the massed pines between Gausse's Hotel des Étrangers and Cannes, five miles away.

from *Tender is the Night* by F. Scott Fitzgerald

● YOUR TURN

In at least 30 lines create an atmosphere of

1.	Menace/Threat	6.	Violence
2.	Happiness	7.	Fear
3.	Terror	8.	Loneliness/Isolation
4.	Suspense	9.	Revulsion/Disgust
5.	Squalor	10.	Solidarity

SUBJECT MATTER

The subject matter of a story is the raw material of character and setting used by the writer. For example, the subject matter of a novel may be working-class life on a Council housing estate, or it might be life in a mining village or it might be life in a general hospital.

Subject matter should not be confused with theme (see page 36 again).

How would you describe the **subject matter** of the following passage?

The schoolmaster was leaving the village, and everybody seemed sorry. The miller at Cresscombe lent him the small white tilted cart and horse to carry his goods to the city of his destination, about twenty miles off, such a vehicle proving of quite sufficient size for the departing teacher's effects. For the school-house had been partly furnished by the managers, and the only cumbersome article possessed by the master, in addition to the packing-case of books, was a cottage piano that he had bought at an auction during the year in which he thought of learning instrumental music. But the enthusiasm having waned he had never acquired any skill in playing, and the purchased article had been a perpetual trouble to him ever since in moving house.

The rector had gone away for the day, being a man who disliked the sight of changes. He did not mean to return till the evening, when the new school-teacher would have arrived and settled in, and everything would be smooth again.

The blacksmith, the farm bailiff, and the school-master himself were standing in perplexed attitudes in the parlour before the instrument.

from *Jude the Obscure* by Thomas Hardy

● YOUR TURN

Identify **ten** kinds of subject matter you have encountered in the fiction you have read.

● THEME

Theme is the meaning or intention that directs and shapes the subject matter of the story. Sometimes it may be a moral lesson such as 'crime does not pay'. Sometimes it may be a certain insight into human experience. The theme of a story is rarely stated explicitly. Usually all the elements of a story must be analysed in order to discover the theme.

In the following extract George Eliot describes the life which the old weaver Silas Marner has been living for the past twenty years in the village of Raveloe.

Previously he had worked in the city and and had belonged to a religious sect that drove him out of the group for a crime he did not commit. In this short passage George Eliot points to the principal theme of her novel. Analyse the passage for the purpose of describing that theme.

> But at last Mrs Osgood's table-linen was finished, and Silas was paid in gold. His earnings in his native town, where he worked for a wholesale dealer, had been after a lower rate; he had been paid weekly, and of his weekly earnings a large proportion had gone to objects of piety and charity. Now, for the first time in his life, he had five bright guineas put into his hand; no man expected a share of them, and he loved no man that he should offer him a share. But what were the guineas to him who saw no vista beyond countless days of weaving? It was needless for him to ask that, for it was pleasant to him to feel them in his palm, and look at their bright faces, which were all his own: it was another element of life, like the weaving and the satisfaction of hunger, subsisting quite aloof from the life of belief and love from which he had been cut off. The weaver's hand had known the touch of hard-won money even before the palm had grown to its full breadth; for twenty years, mysterious money had stood to him as the symbol of earthly good, and the immediate object of toil. He had seemed to love it little in the years when every penny had its purpose for him; for he loved the *purpose* then. But now, when all purpose was gone, the habit of looking towards the money and grasping it with a sense of fulfilled effort made a loam that was deep enough for the seeds of desire; and as Silas walked homeward across the fields in the twilight, he drew out the money and thought it was brighter in the gathering gloom.

from *Silas Marner* by George Eliot

● YOUR TURN

Write a list of what you consider to be the commonest **ten** themes in the fiction you have read.

DIALOGUE

Dialogue serves two main purposes:
- To supply the reader with information about a character or characters
- To advance the plot by supplying necessary information

Although these two purposes can be achieved in other ways, dialogue is often a more dramatic and interesting way of doing this.

From the dialogue in the following passage, what impression do you form of the old fisherman Santiago and the boy? And what do you learn about their relationship?

He was an old man who fished alone in a skiff in the Gulf Stream and he had gone eighty-four days now without taking a fish. In the first forty days a boy had been with him. But after forty days without a fish the boy's parents had told him that the old man was now definitely and finally *salaō*, which is the worst form of unlucky, and the boy had gone at their orders in another boat which caught three good fish the first week. It made the boy sad to see the old man come in each day with his skiff empty and he always went down to help him carry either the coiled lines or the gaff and harpoon and the sail that was furled around the mast. The sail was patched with flour sacks and, furled, it looked like the flag of permanent defeat.

The old man was thin and gaunt with deep wrinkles in the back of his neck. The brown blotches of the benevolent skin cancer the sun brings from its reflection on the tropic seas were on his cheeks. The blotches ran well down the sides of his face and his hands had the deep-creased scars from handling heaving fish on the cords. But none of these scars were fresh. They were as old as erosions in a fishless desert.

Everything about him was old except his eyes and they were the same colour as the sea and were cheerful and undefeated.

'Santiago,' the boy said to him as they climbed the bank from where the skiff was hauled up. 'I could go with you again. We've made some money.'

The old man had taught the boy to fish and the boy loved him.

'No,' the old man said. 'You're with a lucky boat. Stay with them.'

'But remember how you went eighty-seven days without fish and then we caught big ones every day for three weeks.'

'I remember,' the old man said. 'I know you did not leave me because you doubted.'

'It was papa made me leave. I am a boy and I must obey him.'

'I know,' the old man said. 'It is quite normal.'

'He hasn't much faith.'

'No,' the old man said. 'But we have. Haven't we?'

'Yes,' the boy said. 'Can I offer you a beer on the Terrace and then we'll take the stuff home.'

'Why not?' the old man said. 'Between fishermen.'

from *The Old Man and The Sea* by Ernest Hemingway

● **YOUR TURN**

(Write at least 30 lines of dialogue for the following situations)

1. Write a dialogue between you and your mother or father which conveys your conflicting views on how both of you see your future.

2. Write a dialogue between a strong character and a weak character which will convey their respective natures.

3. Write a dialogue between you and an angry neighbour who has called to your house to complain about the loud music you have been playing.

4. Write a dialogue between you and a friend of yours who has decided to break off a relationship with a boyfriend/girlfriend.

5. Write a dialogue that occurs among three or four people who are planning to do something dangerous. The dialogue should convey an impression of the characters and also what they are planning to do.

6. Write a dialogue between two characters which contains only hints of an action they are planning.

7. Write a dialogue between a kidnapper and his or her victim. The dialogue should convey an impression of the characters and also the situation in which they find themselves.

DESCRIPTION

Description may be factual or emotive. Both kinds are used in fiction. What is important is to analyse the writer's intention in making his or her selection of the descriptive details, to ask oneself, for instance, why, of all the things a writer could say about a character or setting, he or she has chosen only certain details.

Comment on the use of similes, metaphors and descriptive details used in the following passage to convey the force and drama of a storm at sea.

A big, foaming sea came out of the mist; it made for the ship, roaring wildly, and in its rush it looked as mischievous and discomposing as a madman with an axe. One or two, shouting, scrambled up the rigging; most, with a convulsive catch of the breath, held on where they stood. Singleton dug his knees under the wheel-box, and carefully eased the helm to the headlong pitch of the ship, but without taking his eyes off the coming wave. It towered close-to and high, like a wall of green glass topped with snow. The ship rose to it as though she had soared on wings, and for a moment rested poised upon the foaming crest as if she had been a great sea-bird. Before we could draw breath a heavy gust struck her, another roller took her unfairly under the weather bow, she gave a toppling lurch, and filled her decks.

from *The Nigger and the Narcissus* by Joseph Conrad

● YOUR TURN

1. Write a description of a party as (a) experienced by someone who has enjoyed it; and (b) as experienced by someone who felt left out.

2. Write a description of a road accident as (a) experienced by someone directly involved; and (b) by an impartial eye-witness.

3. Write an emotive description of a character you dislike.

4. Write a description of your friend's house to convey your dislike of your friend's parents.

5. Write a factual description of your average schoolday.

6. Write a description of a social function (such as a birthday party) which you attended. Make it convey your warm feelings towards your friend.

7. Write a factual description of a family row.

8. Write a description of your sister's boyfriend that conveys your dislike of him.

9. Write a description of a public figure that conveys your admiration of that person.

10. Write an objective/factual description of the area where you live.

ELEMENTS OF FICTION IN PRACTICE

The following short story by James Joyce affords an excellent opportunity of seeing how a master writer uses the various elements of fiction. What Joyce does in miniature in the short story is attempted by the novelist on a larger scale in the writing of novels.

A PAINFUL CASE BY JAMES JOYCE

Mr James Duffy lived in Chapelizod because he wished to live as far away as possible from the city of which he was a citizen and because he found all the other suburbs of Dublin mean, modern and pretentious. He lived in an old sombre house and from his windows he could look into the disused distillery or upwards along the shallow river on which Dublin is built. The lofty walls of his uncarpeted room were free from pictures. He had himself bought every article of furniture in the room: a black iron bedstead, an iron washstand, four cane chairs, a clothes-rack, a coal-scuttle, a fender and irons and a square table on which lay a double desk. A bookcase had been made in an alcove by means of shelves of white wood. The bed was clothed with white bedclothes and a black and scarlet rug covered the foot. A little hand-mirror hung above the washstand and during the day a white-shaded lamp stood as the sole ornament on the mantelpiece. The books on the white wood shelves were arranged from below upwards according to bulk. A complete Wordsworth stood at one end of the lowest shelf and a copy of the *Maynooth Catechism*, sewn into the cloth cover of a notebook, stood at one end of the top shelf. Writing materials were always on the desk. In the desk lay a manuscript translation of Hauptmann's *Michael Kramer*, the stage directions of which were written in purple ink, and a little sheaf of papers held together by a brass pin. In these sheets a sentence was inscribed from time to time and, in an ironical moment, the headline of an advertisement for *Bile Beans* had been pasted on to the first sheet. On lifting the lid of the desk a faint fragrance escaped — the fragrance of new cedar-wood pencils or of a bottle of gum or of an over-ripe apple which might have been left there and forgotten.

Mr Duffy abhorred anything which betokened physical or mental disorder. A medieval doctor would have called him saturnine. His face, which carried the entire tale of his years, was of the brown tint of Dublin streets. On his long and rather large head grew dry black hair and a tawny moustache did not quite cover an unamiable mouth. His cheekbones also gave his face a harsh character; but there was no harshness in the eyes which, looking at the world from under their tawny eyebrows, gave the impression of a man ever alert to greet a redeeming instinct in others but often disappointed. He lived at a little distance from his body, regarding his own acts with doubtful side-glances. He had an odd autobiographical habit which led him to compose in his mind from time to time a short sentence about himself containing a subject in the third person and a predicate in the past tense. He never gave alms to beggars and walked firmly, carrying a stout hazel.

He had been for many years cashier of a private bank in Baggot Street. Every morning he came in from Chapelizod by tram. At midday he went to Dan Burke's and look his lunch — a bottle of lager beer and a small trayful of arrowroot biscuits. At four o'clock he was set free. He dined in an eating-house in George's Street where he felt safe from the society of Dublin's gilded youth and where there was a certain plain honesty in the bill of fare. His evenings were spent either before his landlady's piano or roaming about the outskirts of the city. His liking for Mozart's music brought him sometimes to an opera or a concert: these were the only dissipations of his life.

He had neither companions nor friends, church nor creed. He lived his spiritual life without any communion with others, visiting his relatives at Christmas and escorting them to the cemetery when they died. He performed these two social duties for old dignity's sake but conceded nothing further to the conventions which regulate the civic life. He allowed himself to think that in certain circumstances he would rob his bank but, as these circumstances never arose, his life rolled out evenly — an adventureless tale.

One evening he found himself sitting beside two ladies in the Rotunda. The house, thinly peopled and silent, gave distressing prophecy of failure. The lady who sat next to him looked round at the deserted house once or twice and then said:

— What a pity there is such a poor house tonight! It's so hard on people to have to sing to empty benches.

He took the remark as an invitation to talk. He was surprised that she seemed so little awkward. While they talked he tried to fix her permanently in his memory. When he learned that the young girl beside her was her daughter he judged her to be a year or so younger than himself. Her face, which must have been handsome, had remained intelligent. It was an oval face with strongly marked features. The eyes were very dark blue and steady. Their gaze began with a defiant note but was confused by what seemed a deliberate swoon of the pupil into the iris, revealing for an instant a temperament of great sensibility. The pupil reasserted itself quickly, this half-disclosed nature fell again under the reign of prudence, and her astrakhan jacket, moulding a bosom of a certain fulness, struck the note of defiance more definitely.

He met her again a few weeks afterwards at a concert in Earlsfort Terrace and seized the moments when her daughter's attention was diverted to became intimate. She alluded once or twice to her husband but her tone was not such as to make the allusion a warning. Her name was Mrs Sinico. Her husband's great-great-grandfather had come from Leghorn. Her husband was captain of a mercantile boat plying between Dublin and Holland; and they had one child.

Meeting her a third time by accident he found courage to make an appointment. She came. This was the first of many meetings; they met always in the evening and chose the most quiet quarters for their walks together. Mr Duffy, however, had a distaste for underhand ways and, finding that they were compelled to meet stealthily, he forced her to ask him to her house. Captain Sinico encouraged his visits, thinking that his daughter's hand was in question. He had dismissed his wife so sincerely from his gallery of pleasures that he did not suspect that anyone else would take an interest in her. As the husband was often away and the daughter out giving music lessons Mr Duffy had many opportunities of enjoying the lady's society. Neither he nor she had had any such adventure before and neither was conscious of any incongruity. Little by little he entangled his thoughts with hers. He lent her books, provided her with ideas, shared his intellectual life with her. She listened to all.

Sometimes in return for his theories she gave out some fact of her own life. With almost maternal solicitude she urged him to let his nature open to the full: she became his confessor. He told her that for some time he had assisted at the meetings of an Irish Socialist Party where he had felt himself a unique figure amidst a score of sober workmen in a garret lit by an inefficient oil-lamp. When the party had divided into three sections, each under its own leader and in its own garret, he had discontinued his attendances. The workmen's discussions, he said, were too timorous; the interest they took in the question of wages was inordinate. He felt that they were hard-featured realists and that they resented an exactitude which was the produce of a leisure not within their reach. No social revolution, he told her, would be likely to strike Dublin for some centuries.

She asked him why he did not write out his thoughts. For what, he asked her, with careful scorn. To compete with phrasemongers, incapable of thinking consecutively for sixty seconds? To submit himself to the criticisms of an obtuse middle class which entrusted its morality to policemen and its fine arts to impresarios?

He went often to her little cottage outside Dublin; often they spent their evenings alone. Little by little, as their thoughts entangled, they spoke of subjects less remote. Her companionship was like a warm soil about an exotic. Many times she allowed the dark to fall upon them, refraining from lighting the lamp. The dark discreet room, their isolation, the music that still vibrated in their ears united them. This union exalted him, wore away the rough edges of his character, emotionalised his mental life. Sometimes he caught himself listening to the sound of his own voice. He thought that in her eyes he would ascend to an angelical stature; and, as he attached the fervent nature of his companion more and more closely to him, he heard the strange impersonal voice which he recognised as his own, insisting on the soul's incurable loneliness. We cannot give ourselves, it said: we are our own. The end of these discourses was that one night during which she had shown every sign of unusual excitement, Mrs. Sinico caught up his hand passionately and pressed it to her cheek.

Mr Duffy was very much surprised. Her interpretation of his words disillusioned him. He did not visit her for a week; then he wrote to her asking her to meet him. As he did not wish their last interview to be troubled by the influence of their ruined confessional they met in a little cake-shop near the Parkgate. It was cold autumn weather but in spite of the cold they wandered up and down the roads of the Park for nearly three hours. They agreed to break off their intercourse: every bond, he said, is a bond to sorrow. When they came out of the Park they walked in silence towards the tram; but here she began to tremble so violently that, fearing another collapse on her part, he bade her good-bye quickly and left her. A few days later he received a parcel containing his books and music.

Four years passed. Mr Duffy returned to his even way of life. His room still bore witness of the orderliness of his mind. Some new pieces of music encumbered the music-stand in the lower room and on his shelves stood two volumes by Nietzsche: *Thus Spake Zarathustra* and *The Gay Science*. He wrote seldom in the sheaf of papers which lay in his desk. One of his sentences, written two months after his last interview with Mrs Sinico, read: Love between man and man is impossible because there must not be sexual intercourse and friendship between man and woman is impossible because there must be sexual intercourse. He kept away from concerts lest he should meet her. His father died; the junior partner of the bank retired. And still every morning he went into the city by tram and every evening walked home from the city after having dined moderately in George's Street and read the evening paper for dessert.

One evening as he was about to put a morsel of corned beef and cabbage into his mouth his hand stopped. His eyes fixed themselves on a paragraph in the evening paper which he had propped against the water-carafe. He replaced the morsel of food on his plate and read the paragraph attentively. Then he drank a glass of water, pushed his plate to one side, doubled the paper down before between his elbows and read the paragraph over and over again. The cabbage began to deposit a cold white grease on his plate. The girl came over to ask him was his dinner not properly cooked. He said it was very good and ate a few mouthfuls of it with difficulty. Then he paid his bill and went out.

He walked along quickly through the November twilight, his stout hazel stick striking the ground regularly, the fringe of the buff *Mail* peeping out of a side-pocket of his tight reefer overcoat. On the lonely road which leads from the Parkgate to Chapelizod he slackened his pace. His stick struck the ground less emphatically and his breath, issuing irregularly, almost with a sighing sound, condensed in the wintry air. When he reached his house he went up at once to his bedroom and, taking the paper from his pocket, read the paragraph again by the failing light of the window. He read it not aloud, but moving his lips as a priest does when he reads the prayers *Secreto*. This was the paragraph:

DEATH OF A LADY AT SYDNEY PARADE

a painful case

To-day at the City of Dublin Hospital the Deputy coroner (in the absence of Mr Leverett) held an inquest on the body of Mrs Emily Sinico, aged forty-three years, who was killed at Sydney Parade Station yesterday evening. The evidence showed that the deceased lady, while attempting to cross the line, was knocked down by the engine of the ten o'clock slow train from Kingstown, thereby sustaining injuries of the head and right side which led to her death.

James Lennon, driver of the engine, stated that he had been in the employment of the railway company for fifteen years. On hearing the guard's whistle he set the train in motion and a second or two afterwards brought it to rest in response to loud cries. The train was going slowly.

P. Dunne, railway porter, stated that as the train was about to start he observed a woman attempting to cross the lines. He ran towards her and shouted, but, before he could reach her, she was caught by the buffer of the engine and fell to the ground.

A juror — You saw the lady fall?

Witness — Yes.

Police Sergeant Croly deposed that when he arrived he found the deceased lying on the platform apparently dead. He had the body taken to the waiting-room pending the arrival of the ambulance.

Constable 57E corroborated.

Dr Halpin, assistant house surgeon of the City of Dublin Hospital, stated that the deceased had two lower ribs fractured and had sustained severe contusions of the right shoulder. The right side of the head had been injured in the fall. The injuries were not sufficient to have caused death in a normal person. Death, in his opinion, had been probably due to shock and sudden failure of the heart's action.

Mr H.B. Patterson Finlay, on behalf of the railway company, expressed his deep regret at the accident. The company had always taken every precaution to prevent people crossing the lines except by the bridges, both by placing notices in every station and by the use of the patent spring gates at level crossings. The deceased had been in the habit of crossing the lines late at night from platform to platform and, in view of certain other circumstances of the case, he did not think the railway officials were to blame.

Captain Sinico, of Leoville, Sydney Parade, husband of the deceased, also gave evidence. He stated that the deceased was his wife. He was not in Dublin at the time of the accident as he had arrived only that morning from Rotterdam. They had been married for twenty-two years and had lived happily until about two years ago when his wife began to be rather intemperate in her habits.

Miss Mary Sinico said that of late her mother had been in the habit of going out at night to buy spirits. She, witness, had often tried to reason with her mother and had induced her to join a league. She was not at home until an hour after the accident.

The jury returned a verdict in accordance with the medical evidence and exonerated Lennon from all blame.

The Deputy Coroner said it was a most painful case, and expressed great sympathy with Captain Sinico and his daughter. He urged on the railway company to take strong measures to prevent the possibility of similar accidents in the future. No blame attached to anyone.

Mr Duffy raised his eyes from the paper and gazed out of his window on the cheerless evening landscape. The river lay quiet beside the empty distillery and from time to time a light appeared in some house on the Lucan road. What an end! The whole narrative of her death revolted him and it revolted him to think that he had ever spoken to her of what he held sacred. The threadbare phrases, the inane expressions of sympathy, the cautious words of a reporter won over to conceal the details of a commonplace vulgar death attacked his stomach. Not merely had she degraded himself; she had degraded him. He saw the squalid tract of her vice, miserable and malodorous. His soul's companion! He thought of the throbbing wretches whom he had seen carrying cans and bottles to be filled by the barman. Just God, what an end! Evidently she had been unfit to live, without any strength of purpose, an easy prey to habits, one of the wrecks on which civilisation has been reared. But that she could have sunk so low! Was it possible he had deceived himself so utterly about her? He remembered her outburst of that night and interpreted it in a harsher sense than he had ever done. He had no difficulty now in approving of the course he had taken.

As the light failed and his memory began to wander he thought her hand touched his. The shock which had at first attacked his stomach was now attacking his nerves. He put on his overcoat and hat quickly and went out. The cold air met him on the threshold; it crept into the sleeves of his coat. When he came to the public-house at Chapelizod Bridge he went in and ordered a hot punch.

The proprietor served him obsequiously but did not venture to talk. There were five or six workingmen in the shop discussing the value of a gentleman's estate in County Kildare. They drank at intervals from their huge pint tumblers and smoked, spitting often on the floor and sometimes dragging the sawdust over their spits with their heavy boots. Mr Duffy sat on his stool and gazed at them, without seeing or hearing them. After a while they went out and he called for another punch. He sat a long time over it. The shop was very quiet. The proprietor sprawled on the counter reading the *Herald* and yawning. Now and again a tram was heard swishing along the lonely road outside.

As he sat there, living over his life with her and evoking alternately the two images in which he now conceived her, he realised that she was dead, that she had ceased to exist, that she had become a memory. He began to feel ill at ease. He asked himself what else could he have done. He could not have carried on a comedy of deception with her; he could not have lived with her openly. He had done what seemed to him best. How was he to blame? Now that she was gone he understood how lonely her life must have been, sitting night after night alone in that room. His life would be lonely too until he, too, died, ceased to exist, became a memory — if anyone remembered him.

It was after nine o'clock when he left the shop. The night was cold and gloomy. He entered the Park by the first gate and walked along under the gaunt trees. He walked through the bleak alleys where they had walked four years before. She seemed to be near him in the darkness. At moments he seemed to feel her voice touch his ear, her hand touch his. He stood still to listen. Why had he withheld life from her? Why had he sentenced her to death? He felt his moral nature falling to pieces.

When he gained the crest of the Magazine Hill he halted and looked along the river towards Dublin, the lights of which burned redly and hospitably in the cold night. He looked down the slope and, at the base, in the shadow of the wall of the Park, he saw some human figures lying. These venal and furtive loves filled him with despair. He gnawed the rectitude of his life; he felt that he had been an outcast from life's feast. One human being had seemed to love him and he had denied her life and happiness: he had sentenced her to ignominy, a death of shame. He knew that the prostrate creatures down by the wall were watching him and wished him gone. No one wanted him; he was outcast from life's feast. He turned his eyes to the grey gleaming river, winding towards Dublin. Beyond the river he saw a goods train winding through the darkness, obstinately and laboriously. It passed slowly out of sight; but still he heard in his ears the laborious drone of the engine reiterating the syllables of his name.

He turned back the way he had come, the rhythm of the engine pounding in his ears. He began to doubt the reality of what memory told him. He halted under a tree and allowed the rhythm to die away. He could not feel her near him in the darkness nor her voice touch his ear. He waited for some minutes listening. He could hear nothing: the night was perfectly silent. He listened again. He felt that he was alone.

COMMENTARY/ ANALYSIS

James Joyce's short story, A Painful Case, illustrates almost all the basic elements of traditional fiction. Although the elements of the story can be isolated and analysed separately, it should always be understood that these elements in the story itself combine to form a unity of effect which is dictated by the theme or artistic intention of the writer. Similarly, the theme of the story can only be appreciated by careful analysis of the elements at work in the story.

SETTING: DESCRIPTIVE DETAILS

In the first paragraph of A Painful Case Joyce focuses the reader's attention on the story's setting. This is where Mr James Duffy lives: the city, the area, the house and even the very room where this character lives. Joyce makes it very clear to the reader that Duffy has himself deliberately chosen where he lives and that even the furnishing of his room are of his own choosing. For this reason we can learn a great deal about the character of Mr Duffy by studying his surroundings and noting carefully the details of description selected by Joyce.

Mr Duffy has chosen to live in an out-of-the-way suburb because he doesn't like the pretentiousness and what he considers the vulgar modernity of the newer and more fashionable suburbs. The house in which he has chosen to lodge is 'an old sombre house'. His room is 'uncarpeted'. No pictures hang on the walls. Joyce deliberately draws the reader's attention to the fact that Duffy 'had bought every article of furniture in the room': the room's furnishings and their arrangement, therefore, should tell the reader something about Duffy. All these articles are basic things. There is no hint of any comfort, not to speak of luxury. These furnishings reflect a frugal, spartan and self-controlled character. Mr Duffy is obviously someone who loves order and tidiness. Even the books on Mr Duffy's book shelves are 'arranged from below upwards according to bulk' (not, note, according to subject matter or author).

CHARACTER

Joyce now proceeds to tell us a little about Duffy's intellectual interests. He has an interest in poetry (he has a copy of the complete poems of William Wordsworth). The manuscript translation (from the German) of Hauptmann's Michael Kramer which Duffy has on his desk, shows that he has a knowledge of German and is up to date in his knowledge of contemporary literature (Michael

Kramer would have been very advanced reading for the time of the story's setting).

From his character's locational setting Joyce now moves in the second paragraph to a description of Duffy's physical appearance and something of his habits. To begin with, Joyce reinforces the impression of Duffy's neatness by informing the reader that he 'abhorred anything which betokened physical or mental disorder'. He is 'saturnine' (that is, cold and gloomy by temperament). His mouth is 'unamiable'. His cheekbones suggest harshness of character. Yet Duffy's eyes are not those of a cold cynic; he still has some hope that people will turn out to be better that he thinks, although he expects to be disappointed. There is a distance between Duffy's mind and his body, clearly indicating that he is not at ease with himself. His lack of charitable feelings has probably more to do with a personal distaste for the 'untidiness' of beggars than with deliberate cruelty.

Joyce now turns to Duffy's social life. The reader is informed that Duffy is a 'cashier in a private bank', which places him socially in the middle class. He takes a frugal lunch in a modest out-of-the-way restaurant. His evenings he spends alone, either playing the piano or going for walks. His only social entertainment is his attendance at an occasional concert or opera. Even on these occasions he keeps to himself.

Duffy is a 'loner' who functions within the social conventions not through conviction of their intrinsic value but simply because they provide him with a means of *regulating* his life. His whole life, in fact, is a regulated dull affair.

PLOT: SITUATION

The plot of Joyce's story only gets underway when Duffy encounters Mrs Sinico at a concert. To his surprise he finds himself responding to this woman. Despite the fact that it is she who opens the conversation, Duffy is evidently attracted by her restrained sensibility.

Duffy and Mrs Sinico meet again by chance some weeks after their first encounter. Mrs Sinico's immediate and frank admission of her marital status suggests that she is not entertaining, at least at this stage, any notion of a romantic affair with Duffy. That, of course, suits Duffy who is attracted solely by the companionship offered by the woman.

The relationship between Duffy and Mrs Sinico develops. Her willingness to listen sympathetically to him provides Duffy with a controlled escape from his solitude. She also flatters his ego by taking his ideas seriously.

PLOT: COMPLICATION

Will the relationship between Duffy and Mrs Sinco remain at a platonic or non-physical level? Duffy seems satisfied to keep things as they are. But what of Mrs Sinico? On introducing her, Joyce has already alerted the reader to her 'temperament of great sensibility'. For all her restraint, therefore, Mrs Sinico is an emotional person, quite the opposite of Duffy.

A time finally arrives when Mrs Sinico suddenly drops the guard of her restraint. One evening, moved deeply by Duffy's conversation, she takes his hand and presses it to her cheek. This is scarcely a great outburst of passion but it is enough to frighten the highly self-controlled Duffy. He believes that she has misunderstood him. Whereas he was contented with her intellectual and social companionship, she was looking for more than this; she was seeking emotional and even physical intimacy. Duffy is shocked and decides to break off his relationship with Mrs Sinico, and this he does without compassion.

PLOT: DEVELOPMENT

Joyce takes events forward by four years. Duffy has not changed during this elapsed time. His life has continued with the same mechanical regularity it always had. Not even his father's death has caused any notable disturbance in the pattern of his regular existence.

But now Duffy suddenly discovers that Mrs Sinico has committed suicide. He tries to remain unmoved by the event; but he is clearly disturbed. The newspaper report supplies him with the squalid circumstances (her alcoholism, etc.) surrounding the suicide. He senses that he is in some way implicated, in some way responsible for what has happened to Mrs Sinico. But in what way? Did he do wrong in breaking off his relationship with her? His initial reaction is to deny this. But he remains disturbed despite his best efforts to rationalise his past behaviour.

PLOT: RESOLUTION

Duffy goes out for a stroll to distract himself. His loneliness, however, envelops him. 'He began to feel ill at ease.' He has no part in the companionship of the pub he visits. And as he passes the lovers in the Phoenix Park, he realises that human love is something from which he has excluded himself. He realises that it is only human love that can break down the barrier of solitude. In cutting Mrs

Sinico out of his life, he was at the same time rejecting the only cure of his essential unhappiness. He has condemned himself to loneliness.

THEME

The theme of Joyce's story is the necessity of human love to human happiness and fulfilment. Love, emotional and physical, is in its nature not a rational business. It is not subject to logical order and control like the arrangement of Duffy's room and his life. It has its own logic: the logic of human need.

Duffy has betrayed life by imposing a mechanical regularity on it. His fear of disorder has made him turn his back not only on love, but on life itself. The price he must pay for this is to remain an outsider, 'an outcast from life's feast'. Duffy is not the superman he likes to think he is. Rather, he is a pathetic emotional cripple.

ATMOSPHERE

The atmosphere of Joyce's story is gloomy and depressing. Joyce's description of Duffy's lodging conveys a sense of joylessness and sterility. Not even Duffy's interest in music enlivens the atmosphere. He has even managed to reduce music to the tedium of his existence.

In the closing paragraphs of the story, Joyce deliberately creates an atmosphere of cheerlessness and lifelessness: the fading light; the cold air creeping up Duffy's coat sleeves; the empty pub; the tram swishing along on the lonely road; the goods train winding through the darkness of the night (perhaps an image of Duffy's life winding through the darkness of his existence); the laborious drone of the engine; the silence of the night.

THE AESTHETIC
USE OF LANGUAGE:
(C) DRAMA

THE ESSENTIAL DRAMA

It is widely believed that drama has its origin in the need for primitive people to create order and meaning out of a chaotic world, and to celebrate that order. To primitive people with no scientific knowledge, not to speak of technology, the workings of nature were mysterious and frightening. Suppose spring never came again? Suppose it never rained again? Suppose the sun did not reappear after an eclipse? Primitive people felt, as we do, the need to control somehow the forces that are thought to be at work in nature. Almost all primitive people act out in their plays the seasonal changes in nature. In doing so they feel that they are exercising some control over these forces. They feel that they can please them or that they can ward off their anger. If nothing else, a sense of protection was felt in this. Initially, this kind of magical control of nature took the form of sympathetic dances and mimetic dance-rituals such as the rain-dances of the North American Indians. The essential conflict of these performances is that between winter and summer. This conflict later broadened out into the conflict between life (summer) and death (winter). In time this essential drama of the struggle between life and death combined with myths and ritualistic dance to develop representational characters of gods and heroes.

THE INDIVIDUAL AND SOCIETY

If the original tension of drama was that between life and death, that tension should also be understood as the tension between order and chaos. The individual was seen as someone who lived in a society which had a distinctive order. That order is maintained by the individual subordinating his or her individual desires to the greater interests of the community represented by the Law (moral code, criminal law, etc.). Only the collective force of the community can dominate the ever-threatening powers of nature. Viewed in this way drama could be seen as a conflict between the desires and behaviour of the individual and the needs of society.

DRAMA & RELIGION: CLASSICAL DRAMA

For the ancient Greeks, the god behind all the phenomena of nature was Dionysus. Festivals were held in honour of this god and at him the ancient Greeks directed their ritualistic hymns and dances. There was a serious aspect to these festivals (including sometimes human sacrifice) as well as a lighter one. The lighter part of the celebration involved people becoming drunk and singing phallic songs and making obscene comments. The Greek word for these proceedings was *komos* from which the word 'comedy' derives. The god Dionysus was usually considered in the form of a goat and the word 'tragedy' in fact means 'goat song'. By the time the Greek writers of tragedy were at work, drama had well evolved from its religious and cultist origins: it had become a formalised art. It told a story (plot), it presented characters, and it had theatrical mechanics such as costumes and masks.

MIRACLE & MYSTERY PLAYS

Before the discovery of Classical drama in the Renaissance, a simple type of drama had developed out of Church ritual. This type of drama was the Miracle or Mystery Play which took as its material scenes that dealt with the birth, death and resurrection of Christ. The purpose of this kind of play was to provide religious instruction to an illiterate society in an interesting way. In time these dramatic presentations became a distraction from Church services proper and they were abandoned by the Church which left their production to the medieval guilds of craftsmen. The Guild of Bakers, for instance, would present *The Last Supper*, and the Guild of Shipwrights would present *The Building of the Ark*. By the fifteenth century this type of dramatic presentation was popular and thriving.

THE MORALITY PLAY

A more developed but still simple type of drama developed out of the Miracle or Mystery Play. This was the Morality Play. The purpose of this kind of play was to teach a moral lesson. Its basic pattern was the struggle between the Virtues and the Vices for the soul of man. The most famous surviving example of a Morality Play is *Everyman* which is believed to have been written in the late fifteenth century. Shakespeare was probably familiar with this kind of drama from his boyhood in Stratford-upon-Avon.

The following is a list of the Dramatis Personae or characters of *Everyman*: Everyman, God (Adonai), Death, Messenger, Fellowship, Cousin, Kindred, Goods, Good-Deeds, Strength, Discretion, Five-Wits, Beauty, Knowledge, Confession, Angel, Doctor.

This is how *Everyman* begins:

Here beginneth a treatise how the high father of Heaven sendeth death to summon every creature to come and give account of their lives in the world and is in manner of a moral play. [Enter a messenger who speaks the Prologue.]

Messenger:

I pray you all give audience,
And hear this matter in reverence,
By figure a moral play:
The *Summoning of Everyman* called it is,
That of our lives and ending shows
How transitory we be all day.
This matter is wondrous precious,
But the intent of it is more gracious,
And sweet to bear away.
The story saith: — Man, in the beginning,
Look well, and take good heed to the ending,
Be you never so gay;
Ye think sin in the beginning full sweet,
Which in the end causeth the soul to weep,

When the body lieth in clay.
Here shall you see how Fellowship and Jollity,
Both Strength, Pleasure, and Beauty,
Will fade from thee as flower of May.
For we shall hear, how our heaven king
Calleth Everyman to a general reckoning:
Give audience, and hear what he doth say.

MODERN DRAMA: THE 'PROBLEM' PLAY

In the twentieth century, theatre has been dominated by the 'problem play'. This kind of play deals with issues arising from modern economic, social and political conditions: unemployment, broken marriage, social isolation, class conflict, etc. The great American playwright, Arthur Miller, has written 'if one could know enough about a human being one could discover some conflict, some value, some challenge ... which he cannot find it in himself to walk away from or turn his back on'. That challenge, that conflict for Miller, as for many modern dramatists, is usually socially rooted. The individual finds himself or herself in a situation in which he or she is at odds with society (often the family).

In Miller's play, *Death of a Salesman*, the central character is Willy Loman, a travelling salesman in his sixties who, having spent his life striving for success, is finally forced by circumstances to face up to the fact of his failure. The company he works for wants to get rid of him. His relationship with his wife and two sons has not been honest. Before this crisis, he believed blindly that if he worked hard and competitively, 'success' would come to him and happiness would follow and his life would be justified. Loman's obsession with success has dehumanised him, forced him to escape from the squalid realities of his life. He has cocooned himself in a web of deceits in which his wife Linda and his sons have colluded. But now he must confront the realities of his life. This is the conflict: he must face up to the failure of his life and apportion blame for it.

THE THEATRE OF IDEAS

Apart from the problem play, which has usually been realistic in form, modern theatre has provided a platform for playwrights who might be called 'philosophical dramatists'. These are writers such as Bertolt Brecht, Samuel Beckett, Eugene Ionesco and Harold Pinter. For these writers, drama is a means for exploring the meaning of life. Characters, plot, props, etc., are exploited as a means to an end. They are not concerned with characters as individual human beings, but as dramatic instruments. In the case of Brecht, their purpose is to illustrate class conflict and to enlighten the audience about the effects of class restrictions upon their lives. In the case of Beckett and Ionesco, the purpose of their drama is to demonstrate, in dramatic terms, the apparent meaninglessness and futility of modern life.

THE MECHANICS OF DRAMA

CHARACTERS

Characterisation is a very important element in a play. Actors must make the characters they portray appear lifelike and credible to an audience. Just like people in actual life, they will have a certain physical appearance, dress in a certain way, speak in a certain way and behave in a certain way according to the values they hold or the personality they have. Their past history may be given or implied in their behaviour and attitudes.

The following is a list of the sort of questions often asked about a character in a play:

1. Age of character? Position in society? Relationships with other characters?

2. Does the character remain consistent throughout the play?

3. Does the character undergo change in the course of the play? Where, how and why does this happen?

4. What values (moral or otherwise) underpin the character? For instance, is the character ruthless, unscrupulous, honest, truthful, deceitful, sadistic, affectionate, confident, insecure, ambitious, etc.?

QUESTIONS

1. Give your impression of the principal character of any play by Shakespeare which you have studied.

2. Discuss the consistency of Shakespeare's portrayal of the main characters in any play of his which you have studied.

3. Discuss a change of character in the hero of any play you have studied. Is this change deliberate? What in your opinion has brought it about?

4. Compare and contrast the values which underpin any character in a play which you have studied.

5. Give your impression of the main characters in any play you have studied.

6. Taking any two conflicting characters in a play you have studied, show how the conflict is
   (a)   One of opposing temperaments
   OR
   (b)   Conflicting interests
   OR
   (c)   Conflicting moral values.

7. Sketch out two dramatic characters (of any play you have studied) which portray the conflict of bigotry and tolerance.

PLOT

Just as in any work of fiction such as a novel or a short story, the plot of a play is its course of action. It is the pattern or shape formed by the events which occur in the play.

SUB-PLOT

The sub-plot is a secondary story-line which is different from the main plot and subordinate to it. It usually helps to emphasise the main plot.

● YOUR TURN

(Write at least 30 lines)

1. Summarise the plot of a play you have studied.

2. Summarise the plot of a film you have seen.

3. Sketch out the plot of a play which will focus on the conflict between youth and age. Use as many characters as you like.

4. Sketch out a plot of a play that also contains a sub-plot. Make the two plots interconnect.

EXPOSITION

As quickly as possible the playwright needs to supply the audience with the information necessary to following what is happening when the play opens. Who are the characters? How do they relate to one another? What situation do they find themselves in?

All this should be done in the *course* of the play, not by stopping the play's action to give this information in bulk. The playwright has to balance the demands of getting the play underway and at the same time supplying the information necessary to make what is happening understandable at once to the audience.

● QUESTIONS

1. Take the opening scene or scenes of any play you have studied, and show how the playwright supplies the information necessary to follow the succeeding events of the play.

2. Why do you think television dramas known as 'soaps' require little or no exposition?

3. For modern plays, a theatre programme usually provides the necessary exposition. Do you think this is a good or bad thing for the play?

4. What dangers do you see for the playwright in providing exposition?

SETTING

Where and when the play's action occurs is the setting of the play. The time and place chosen will affect the mood and atmosphere of a play.

QUESTIONS

1. Discuss in detail the appropriateness of the setting of the opening scene of any play you have studied.

2. Comment on the effectiveness of the opening scene of any Shakespearian play you have studied.

3. Give an example of what you would consider a mismatch of setting and the dramatic action which occurs in it.

4. With reference to any play you have studied, comment on the contribution of the setting of any event to the dramatic action that occurs.

DIALOGUE

In a play, dialogue is even more important than in a novel or a short story. The main function of dialogue, combined with action, is to express character. The nature of a character should always be heard through that character's dialogue. Dialogue also can be used to supply expository matter and to develop the plot.

QUESTIONS

1. Take any piece of dialogue from a play you have studied and show how it illustrates the nature of the characters who speak.

2. Show how a piece of dialogue can add to our understanding of some aspect of the plot of a play you have studied.

3. Write a piece of dialogue that will convey the impression of a ruthless new boss attempting to get rid of an old loyal worker.

4. Mime is drama without dialogue. In what ways do you think this limits the scope of mime?

THEME

The theme of a play is the message, moral or insight into human behaviour which the playwright wishes to communicate to the audience. It is usually the controlling element in the play, determining character, plot and the nature of the conflict. Often the theme of a play is not explicitly stated and can only be worked out by analysing the various elements of the play. The theme of a play might be the evils of war, the importance of love and affection, the individual in conflict with society, for example.

● QUESTIONS

1. Taking any play you have studied, show how character, plot and setting combine to point to the play's central theme.

2. Taking any scene from a play you have studied, analyse the clues by which you have discovered the theme of the play.

3. In what part of any play which you have studied have you found the theme of the play to be most forcibly stated or implied?

4. Make a list of the themes of at least five plays or films you have seen.

CONFLICT

Conflict is the essence of drama. Conflict may be between characters of different temperament and personality, characters who hold different values or viewpoints; or conflict may be between characters and a situation in which they find themselves, as for instance, a group of characters who find themselves in a survival situation (a plane crash, a kidnapping, poverty, for example).

● QUESTIONS

1. Taking any scene from any play you have studied, show how the nature of the conflict emerges from the scene.

2. Discuss the nature of the conflict between any two characters in a play you have studied.

3. Taking any play you have studied, describe the nature of the conflict that gives the play its unity.

4. Make out a list of as many situations of conflict as you can imagine. You may refer to plays, films or novels you have experienced.

5. Why do you think that conflict is at the very heart of drama?

SUSPENSE

Just as in a novel or a short story, a play must maintain the interest of the audience, and suspense has an important function in doing this. A sense of tension will be created in the audience as they anticipate the outcome of a situation. For instance, in a conflict between two characters, the outcome of the conflict may be held back to the last possible moment (the climax). Almost all television 'soaps' are based on suspense: every instalment of the 'soap' tries to leave the audience curious and guessing about what will take place next.

The setting of a play often contributes to suspense. A character finds himself or herself in a house where he or she discovers a corpse. Has the person been murdered? Is the murderer still in the house? Most detective plays or thrillers are based on the creation of suspense about the identity of the murderer.

QUESTIONS

1. Using any play you have studied, select any three turns in the play's plot that are calculated to create suspense.

2. Although plot is the main means of creating suspense, character can also be used for this purpose. Illustrate this with reference to any play you have studied.

3. For what reasons do you think suspense is often considered very important to dramatic action?

4. Would you consider suspense more important in tragedy than in comedy? Give reasons for your answer.

CLIMAX

The moment when the action of a play reaches the highest point of intensity is called the climax. Will the hero be killed? Will the murderer at last be discovered? Will the kidnap victim be released unharmed? The climax usually occurs at the end of a play.

● QUESTIONS

1. Identify and describe any scenes in a play you have studied that involve moments of climax?

2. Identify and analyse the climax of any play you have studied.

3. What function in your opinion does the creation of suspense play in bringing about the climactic moment in a play?

4. What do you consider to be the main function of climax so far as the audience is concerned?

RESOLUTION (OR DÉNOUEMENT)

The resolution of a play is the way the situation is sorted out after the climax has passed. In a fairytale, for example, the resolution is usually the simple 'And they lived happily ever after.' Or it may be that the good characters are rewarded and the villains punished.

● QUESTIONS

1. Take the plot of any play you have studied and show how its plot is finally resolved.

2. Why do you think an audience would be disappointed with a play that ends without resolution of its dramatic action?

3. Can you see any reason why a playwright might leave the dramatic action of a play unresolved?

4. Why do you think audiences generally are more pleased with a happy resolution than with a sad one?

CLASSICAL TRAGEDY

OEDIPUS THE KING BY SOPHOCLES: THE TRAGIC MODEL

Background

For the Greeks, Apollo was the supreme deity, the origin of everything valued by them, the foundation of their civilisation. He presided over law, the arts, sports, all moral, social and cultural values. He was known as Loxias, the Healer. He was associated with Phoebus the sun-god and hence he has associations with light and goodness.

Apollo's most important function was to protect the moral and social order of the state. He was the supreme legislator in cases of murder because murder was viewed as the most serious threat to society. Regicide (the murder of a king) was considered the ultimate menace because it could reduce the whole of society to chaos. Murder corrupted society. Apollo had the right to punish the criminal and by so doing he purged society and restored it to health.

Apollo would let his voice and judgement be heard through oracles, the most famous of which was at Delphi. To this oracle all important social and moral questions were addressed. So important was this oracle at Delphi that the Greeks believed Delphi was the centre or 'navel' of the earth.

KING OEDIPUS

In Sophocles' *Oedipus the King*, the fate of the hero Oedipus is controlled by Apollo from the very beginning. It is Apollo, through his oracle, who decrees that Oedipus will kill his father, marry his mother and bring misfortune on his family and society. This is his fate. The purpose of the tragedy is to show how it is useless to try to escape one's fate. Innocent though he is in not being aware of the nature of his crimes, Oedipus must submit to the gods and their punishment. Only in so doing can society be purged of the corruption he has brought on it. Only then can Loxias the Healer cure the 'plague' which Oedipus has brought on society.

The focus of *Oedipus the King* is on the gradual revelation of truth which will result in awareness and punishment and purification. Apollo's presence is felt throughout the play. He will shed light on the darkness (crimes). At the beginning of the play, Oedipus believes he is invulnerable, that the truth cannot harm him, that he can see the truth. But he is really blind. Ironically, by the end of the play, when he has been dragged down by suffering and is physically blind, Oedipus comes to see the truth. In accepting the justice of his guilt and punishment, he is spiritually restored to goodness and the city of Thebes is restored by Apollo to moral, social and political order. Wisdom is learnt through suffering, goodness through evil.

From OEDIPUS THE KING by SOPHOCLES*

Plot:

Many years before the events of the play begin, Oedipus came as a stranger to the city of Thebes. There he found that the Theban king Laios had been killed and that the city was plagued by a monster, the Sphinx. This monster would only cease its destruction when someone answered the riddle: What first goes on four feet, then on two and finally on three? The correct answer, given by Oedipus, was a human being, who as a baby crawls on all four limbs, walks on two and in old age needs the support of a stick. The monster destroyed itself and the citizens of Thebes made Oedipus their king. He then married Jocasta, the widow of Laios.

However, plague has once more come upon the city and its citizens once again are seeking the help of Oedipus. What Oedipus does not know is that he is the son of the dead king Laios whom he unwittingly killed on his way to Thebes, and that in marrying the dead king's widow, Jocasta, he has married his mother. It is this sin of Oedipus that has finally brought plague on the city. In the course of the play, he will become aware of his guilt and undergo the punishment that is necessary to purge himself and the city of Thebes of the evil he has brought upon it.

Characters:

Oedipus: King of Thebes
Priest of Apollo
Creon: the brother of Jocasta

SCENE. *Before the palace of Oedipus, King of Thebes. A central door and two lateral doors open onto a platform which runs the length of the facade. On the platform, right and left, are altars; and three steps lead down into the 'orchestra', or chorus-ground. At the beginning of the action these steps are crowded with*

---

*from *The Oedipus Cycle*, trans. by Dudley Fitts and Robert Fitzgerald (Harcourt, Brace and World)

suppliants who have brought branches and chaplets of olive leaves and who lie in various attitudes of despair. OEDIPUS enters.

PROLOGUE

OEDIPUS:
My children, generations of the living
In the line of Kadmos, nursed at his ancient hearth:
Why have you strewn yourselves before these altars
In supplication, with your boughs and garlands?
The breath of incense rises from the city
With a sound of prayer and lamentation.
                          Children,
I would not have you speak through messengers,
And therefore I have come myself to hear you —
I, Oedipus, who bear the famous name.
[*To a* PRIEST]
You, there, since you are the eldest in the company,
Speak for them all, tell me what preys upon you,
Whether you come in dread, or crave some blessing:
Tell me, and never doubt that I will help you
In every way I can; I should be heartless
Were I not moved to find you suppliant here.
PRIEST:
Great Oedipus, O powerful King of Thebes!
You see how all the ages of our people
Cling to your altar steps: here are boys
Who can barely stand alone, and here are priests
By weight of age, as I am a priest of God,
And young men chosen from those yet unmarried;
As for the others, all that multitude,
They wait with olive chaplets in the squares,
At the two shrines of Pallas, and where Apollo
Speaks in the glowing embers.
                        Your own eyes
Must tell you: Thebes is tossed on a murdering sea

And can not lift her head from the death surge.
A rust consumes the buds and fruits of the earth;
The herds are sick; children die unborn,
And labour is vain. The god of plague and pyre
Raids like detestable lightning through the city,
And all the house of Kadmos is laid waste,
All emptied, and all darkened: Death alone
Battens upon the misery of Thebes.

You are not one of the immortal gods, we know;
Yet we have come to you to make our prayer
As to the man surest in mortal ways
And wisest in the ways of God. You saved us
From the Sphinx, that flinty singer, and the tribute
We paid to her so long; yet you were never
Better informed than we, nor could we teach you:
It was some god breathed in you to set us free.

Therefore, O mighty King, we turn to you:
Find us our safety, find us a remedy,
Whether by counsel of the gods or men.
A king of wisdom tested in the past
Can act in a time of troubles, and act well.
Noblest of men, restore
Life to your city! Think how all men call you
Liberator for your trouble long ago;
Ah, when your years of kingship are remembered,
Let them not say *We rose, but later fell* —
Keep the state from going down in the storm!
Once, years ago, with happy augury,
You brought us fortune; be the same again!
No man questions your power to rule the land:
But rule over men, not over a dead city!
Ships are only hulls, citadels are nothing,
When no life moves in the empty passageways.

OEDIPUS:

Poor children! You may be sure I know

All that you longed for in your coming here.

I know that you are deathly sick; and yet,

Sick as you are, not one is as sick as I.

Each of you suffers in himself alone

His anguish, not another's; but my spirit

Groans for the city, for myself, for you.

I was not sleeping, you are not waking me.

No, I have been in tears for a long while

And in my restless thoughts walked many ways.

In all my search, I found one helpful course,

And that I have taken: I have sent Creon,

Son of Menoikeus, brother of the queen,

To Delphi, Apollo's place of revelation,

To learn there, if he can,

What act or pledge of mine can save the city.

I have counted the days, and now, this very day,

I am troubled, for he has overstayed his time.

What is he doing? He has been gone too long.

Yet whenever he comes back, I should do ill

To scant whatever duty God reveals.

PRIEST:

It is a timely promise. At this instant

They tell me Creon is here.

OEDIPUS:

                          O Lord Apollo!

May his news be fair as his face is radiant!

PRIEST:

It could not be otherwise: he is crowned with bay,

The chaplet is thick with berries.

OEDIPUS:

                         We shall soon know;

He is near enough to hear us now.

[*Enter* CREON]

O Prince:

Brother: son of Menoikeus:

What answer do you bring to us from the god?

CREON:

A strong one. I can tell you, great afflictions

Will turn out well, if they are taken well.

OEDIPUS:

What was the oracle? These vague words.

QUESTIONS

1. Basing your answer on the extract, do you think that Oedipus was mistaken in his belief in the 'gods'?

2. What role do you think the Priest plays in this extract?

3. Give your impression of the character of Creon.

4. Discuss the idea that fate or destiny must be accepted. Base your discussion on the extract.

5. Discuss the use of irony that runs throughout the extract. What is the dramatic effect of this irony?

6. Do you think that people today can learn anything from this extract?

AN APPROACH TO SHAKESPEARE

The central conflict in all of Shakespeare's great tragedies is, like that of Classical Greek drama and the Morality Play, to which they owe a great deal, the struggle between good and evil. The nature of good and evil in Shakespeare needs to be understood in some detail.

GOOD

Good in Shakespeare may be given the name of Christian humanism. Essentially, this is the code of moral values taught by the Christian Church down through the centuries. It held that God had created a meaningful world in which everything and everyone had a natural place in the scheme of things. At its creation, laws were implanted by God into this world and the controlling principle of these laws was Nature. This Nature is not the apparently blind force of Darwinian evolution. It is a meaningful, divine control. Only human beings, by virtue of their free will, can act contrary to Nature. Nature, unobstructed by human beings, results in Order. If human beings behave naturally, in this special sense of Nature, that is, according to God's plan for them revealed by the Bible and by Church philosophers, then there will be order in society and human beings can achieve their purpose in life — spiritual salvation.

EVIL

This vision of a divinely ordered universe was challenged in Shakespeare's time by the sceptical writings of Giordano Bruno (1548–1600), Niccolò Machiavelli (1459–1527) and Michel de Montaigne (1533–1592). These writers questioned theological and Church authority. They sought to explain human history and natural phenomena without reference to a controlling divinity. Their view of the world is recognisably modern. People are driven by their needs, by their ambitions. Life is a constant struggle, and success and failure are determined by talent, cunning, chance and power. In the eyes of Christian humanists at the time, this scepticism was a terrifying threat to a stable social order fixed on a commonly accepted morality.

KINGSHIP IN SHAKESPEARE

To illustrate the conflict of these opposing views, one can turn to Shakespeare's *Hamlet* and *King Lear*. In *Hamlet*, Laertes is warning his sister Ophelia not to become romantically involved with Prince Hamlet. He says

> .... you must fear,
> His greatness weigh'd, his will is not his own.
> For he himself is subject to his birth:
> He may not, as unvalu'd persons do,
> Carve for himself, for on his choice depends
> The sanity and health of this whole state;
> And therefore must his choice be circumscrib'd
> Unto the voice and yielding of that Body
> Whereof he is the head.

(I.ii.16–24)

Here, as in numerous passages in Shakespeare's plays, is the notion of kingship as a divinely ordained role. Through the legitimate king, God exercises his benevolent influence on society. The legitimate king may possess absolute power in human affairs but he is morally circumscribed by the higher authority of God. His rejection of that higher authority would make him a tyrant, a ruler who exercises absolute power for the gratification of his own ambitions.

THE TYRANT

In contrast to this notion of legitimate kingship there is the opposing view expressed clearly by Edmund in Shakespeare's *King Lear*. Edmund is the illegitimate son of the Earl of Gloucester. According to the moral and social code of Christian humanism, Edmund, through his illegitimacy, would be debarred from the inheritance which should naturally fall to his step-brother Edgar, the older and legitimate son of Gloucester. In the following speech, Edmund is questioning the Nature that ordains things so. His own view of Nature, which is the nature he addresses in the opening line, is that of a purely physical force.

> Thou, Nature, art my goddess; to thy law
> My services are bound. Wherefore should I
> Stand in the plague of custom, and permit
> The curiosity of nations to deprive me,
> For that I am some twelve or fourteen moonshines
> Lag of a brother? Why bastard? Wherefore base?
> When my dimensions are as well compact,
> My mind as generous, and my shape as true,
> As honest madam's issue? Why brand they us
> With base? with baseness? bastardy? base, base?
> Who in the lusty stealth of nature take
> More composition and fierce quality
> Than doth, within a dull, stale, tired bed,
> Go to th'creating a whole tribe of fops,
> Got 'tween asleep and wake? Well then,
> Legitimate Edgar, I must have your land:
> Our father's love is to the bastard Edmund
> As to th'legitimate.

(I.ii.1–18)

THE TRAGIC PATTERN

The basic dramatic pattern that is common to Shakespeare's tragedies is that of the Fall and Redemption of man. This derives from the primal story of Adam and Eve who symbolise humanity at large.

- They are tempted to evil
- They yield to the temptation and make a wrong moral choice
- They are punished
- Through their punishment they become aware of their guilt
- They are purged of their sin through their suffering
- They are forgiven through God's mercy
- They achieve or have the hope of salvation

In his different tragedies, Shakespeare's focus is concentrated on different stages of this primal story. In *Hamlet,* for example, the focus is on the process of Hamlet's moral growth into the knowledge of his own weakness (it is through this knowledge that he will achieve salvation). In *Othello*, the focus of the play is on the making of the wrong moral choice which will bring about Othello's downfall. In *King Lear*, Shakespeare concentrates on the process of spiritual renewal after Lear has made a wrong moral choice. In *Macbeth*, Shakespeare is preoccupied with the terrifying workings of evil.

SHAKESPEARE'S THEATRE & CHARACTERS

Shakespeare's plays combine realism and symbolism. Their characters are individualised in order to make them credible to the audience. But they are not to be mistaken for real people. The audience has no business being concerned about details of their lives which have no bearing on the thematic pattern of the play. So far as realism goes, it is enough that the characters behave with consistency. For all their lifelike qualities, characters in a Shakespearian play are not psychological case-studies. They are dramatic embodiments of moral values. Shakespeare's primary interest is to explore the moral dimension of human experience — the struggle between good and evil. *Macbeth*, for example, is not the story of a murder gone wrong. It is a study in the operation of the force of evil that ever threatens the human soul with damnation. Similarly, *King Lear* is not the story of a foolish old king who is the innocent victim of his daughters' ingratitude. Rather, it is a study in how vanity and moral immaturity in a king can bring chaos on the society for whose order he is morally responsible.

GLOSSARY OF
LITERARY TERMS

aesthetics: the study of artistic beauty.

allegory: a story which has a parallel meaning to which it refers at every point; the characters, objects and events stand for other things in that parallel meaning.

alliteration: the repetition on consonantal sounds, usually at the beginning of two or three consecutive words. E.g. <u>F</u>ull <u>f</u>athoms <u>f</u>ive thy <u>f</u>ather lies.

allusion: reference to a person, place, event or area of knowledge such as classical mythology.

analogy: a loose comparison, based only on a partial resemblance. E.g. comparing the course of a human life to that of a river: a stream developing into a river that makes its way to the sea.

antagonist: the character or force that opposes the main character (the protagonist) as he or she attempts to resolve the conflict of the problem/situation that is at the centre of the drama.

anti-climax: an outcome of events which is surprisingly different from what was expected; it is often humorous in its effect.

aphorism: a compressed statement of a truth, such 'He who hesitates shall be lost'.

assonance: vowel rhyme. E.g.

> When the bl*a*ck herds of the r*ai*n were gr*a*zing
>
> In the g*a*p of the pure cold wind
>
> And the watery h*a*zes of the h*a*zel
>
> Brought her into my mind ...
>
> — Austin Clarke

atmosphere: the feeling of a scene in a literary work, created by mood, setting and anticipation.

biography: the life of a person written by someone other than that person.

blank verse: verse without rhyme, usually iambic pentameters as in Shakespeare's plays.

cadence: a musical rising and falling rhythm.

character: a person in a work of fiction; can also be an animal or an object.

characterisation: the technique of portraying a fictional character.

classicism: possessing the qualities of the art of ancient Greece and Rome: clean objectivity, proportion and balance, restraint and nobility; in contrast to romanticism which is thought of as subjective, vague, disordered, etc.

cliché: a phrase or expression drained of life by excessive use. E.g. 'When he saw me, *he let his guard down*.'

climax: the highest point of intensity in a literary work, after which the reader is sure about the outcome of the action.

coincidence: the accidental occurrence of two or more events at the same time; usually considered a weakness when it is found in a plot.

conflict: the struggle between opposing forces, characters, ideas or beliefs which is the focus of the plot; the outcome of conflict is the victory of one side over the other, usually of good over evil.

connotation: the emotional associations which words and phrases have; they are brought into play by suggestion.

consonance: the rhyming of consonantal sounds, such as *flip-flop*.

contrast: comparison used to highlight different rather than similarity.

couplet: two lines of poetry that rhyme; the heroic couplet — in which almost all the poetry of the 18th century in English was written — consists of two lines of iambic pentameter rhymed.

denotation: the dictionary or literal definition of a word.

dénouement: the working out of the plot — the sorting out of events — after the climax has been reached.

dialect: speech peculiar to a specific region; not standard speech.

dialogue: the speech of characters in a work of fiction.

didactic: moralising, preaching a lesson.

dissonance: harsh, clashing sound.

elegy: a poem of lament or sadness.

epigram: a compressed saying. E.g. 'It is better to light one candle than curse the dark.'

episode: an incident or sub-section of the main plot.

essay: a short composition usually personal in subject matter or treatment.

euphemism: a polite way of expressing something otherwise offensive. E.g. We had the dog *put to sleep*.

exposition: the background information necessary to understand the situation with which the literary work begins.

fantasy: a work that is clearly incredible; it can be entertaining in an escapist manner.

figure of speech: the name given to a technique of language, such as similes etc., which is used in literary writing.

flashback: the recalling of some previous incident or event and bringing it into relationship with the present time.

foreshadowing: clues or hints in anticipation of what is to come.

form: the metrical or prosodic structure of a poem; the over-all structure of a literary work.

free verse: poetry not written in accordance with traditional metrics or a fixed pattern but written to please the uncoded sense of hearing.

humour: the source of amusement, laughter, comedy; it can be found in character, situation, presentation, etc.

hyperbole: gross exaggeration usually for comic effect.

idiom: the use of expressions peculiar to a particular language.

image: a mental picture or impression of something external; the combination of details to represent a particular thing.

incident: usually a minor event in the over-all course of action in a work of fiction.

irony: a manner of saying something which means the opposite of what is actually stated, as, for example — to indicate meanness — 'He spent money like royalty!'; it can also be used to describe an outcome of a situation which is the opposite of what is expected.

legend: an ancient story that may or may not have a basis in historical fact.

lyric: a short subjective poem expressing emotion.

melodrama: a simplistic and unsophisticated kind of drama in which feelings are exaggerated; the bad are very bad and the good are very good and there is no grey area between.

metaphor: a comparison made without using the words 'like' and 'as'; *metaphorical* means not literally true.

metaphysical: refers to a certain kind of poetry written in the late 16th and 17th centuries which makes frequent use of elaborate, intellectual comparisons.

metre: the measurement of verse into feet or units of rhythm.

mock epic: a long narrative poem that uses the features of the classical epic, such as grandeur and exaggeration, for comic effect.

mood: a condition of mind and emotion such as sadness or happiness, created by literary writing.

moral: the message, lesson or instruction taught by the work.

motivation: the driving or controlling force within a character.

movement: a literary group-development i.e., a group of writers who favour a certain style of writing.

narrator: the person who relates an event or events; when a story is told in the first person ('I' or 'We") the narrative is said to be a first person narrative; otherwise, it is a third person narrative.

ode: usually, a long lyric poem expressing effusive praise for someone or something.

onomatopeia: the imitation by sound of the thing referred to, such 'the *flash* of lightning'.

paradox: an apparently contradictory statement which is not in fact so. E.g. 'The sinner must first die in order to live [i.e. to live in grace].'

paraphrase: rephrasing the meaning of something in one's own words.

parody: a comic imitation of a serious work or style.

pastoral: an idealised presentation of a rural setting and characters, usually shepherds and shepherdesses.

pathetic fallacy: the treatment of an inanimate thing as though it were human. E.g. 'O wild West Wind, thou breath of Autumn's being'.

pathos: a quality in a literary work that stirs the feeling of pity or compassion.

personification: the treatment of places and things as if they possessed human qualities.

plot: the pattern of the course of action of a work of fiction.

poetic justice: the wicked are punished and the good are rewarded in response to how the reader would like the outcome to be.

protagonist: the main character of a literary work, who embodies the conflict that forms the core the work.

pun: a play on words that exploits more than one meaning of a word. E.g. 'It must be admitted that he spoke *gravely* when on the point of death.' ['gravely' here means 'seriously' as well as referring to the 'grave'.]

resolution: the unravelling of events after the climax has been reached.

rhetorical question: a question that implies its answer (thus, not a genuine question simply asking for information). E.g. 'If this be life, how welcome must death be?'

rhyme: syllables that have the same sound, as 'hat', 'cat', 'that'.

rhyme scheme: a regular pattern of rhymes.

rhythm: the pattern of sound in verse or prose.

romance: a narrative that deals with adventures of chivalry.

romantic: the opposite of 'classical'; imaginative and subjective as opposed to rational and objective.

satire: a form of criticism by means of ridicule and mockery.

sentimentality: a display of emotion in excess of what would normally be considered appropriate.

setting: the time and place in which the action of a work of fiction occurs.

simile: a comparison introduced by the word 'like' or 'as'.

soliloquy: a speech spoken by a character in a play in which he or she is speaking to himself or herself but is, of course, heard by the audience though not by the other characters in the play.

sonnet: a form of poem consisting of fourteen lines of iambic pentameter; these lines may be divided into two groups of octave and sestet (a Petrarchan sonnet, with the rhyme scheme: ABBAABBA CDCDCD) or three groups of quatrains and a couplet (a Shakespearian sonnet, with the rhyme scheme: ABAB CDCD EFEF GG).

stereotype: a character or situation that conforms to a generalisation. E.g. Scrooge as a stereotype of the miser.

structure: the pattern of organisation of a literary work.

style: the characteristic features of a writer's use of language or of a work.

sub-plot: a secondary story-line that is subordinate to the main plot but usually contributes to it.

suspense: an acute sense of anticipation about the outcome of a situation.

symbol: that which stands for something other than itself.

theme: the 'message', idea or insight that is the controlling principle of a literary work and to which all other elements of the work are usually subordinated.

tone: the writer's attitude towards the reader and towards the subject matter of the work.

tragedy: a kind of drama in which the main character is subjected to a conflict that has as its outcome the defeat of the character but also, usually, an heroic display of the human spirit.

verisimilitude: true to life in all respects.